FULL OF MYS

FULL *of* MYSELF

BLACK WOMANHOOD
and the JOURNEY
to SELF-POSSESSION

Austin Channing Brown

CONVERGENT

NEW YORK

Convergent
An imprint of Random House
A division of Penguin Random House LLC
1745 Broadway, New York, NY 10019
convergentbooks.com
penguinrandomhouse.com

Hardcover ISBN 978-0-593-72836-9
Ebook ISBN 978-0-593-72837-6

Printed in the United States of America on acid-free paper

convergentbooks.com

1st Printing

FIRST EDITION

Book design by Barbara M. Bachman

BOOK TEAM: MANAGING EDITOR: *Allison Fox* • PRODUCTION
MANAGER: *Sarah Feightner* • COPYEDITOR: *Susan M. S. Brown* •
PROOFREADERS: *Kellyn Readdy, Pam Rehm*

The authorized representative in the EU for product safety
and compliance is Penguin Random House Ireland, Morrison
Chambers, 32 Nassau Street, Dublin D02 YH68, Ireland.
https://eu-contact.penguin.ie.

For every Black woman
holding herself together with both hands

and he said: you pretty full of yourself ain't chu
so she replied: show me someone not full of herself
and i'll show you a hungry person

—NIKKI GIOVANNI,
"POEM FOR A LADY WHOSE
VOICE I LIKE"

Contents

Foreword

> The fact is that anybody who has survived
> his childhood has enough information about life
> to last him the rest of his days.
>
> —FLANNERY O'CONNOR

LET'S BEGIN WITH our beginning. Austin Channing Brown and I met in person for the first time at a little restaurant next to the beach. It was lunchtime, but the dining room was just opening. We chose to sit outside where we could feel the sun on our skin and hear how close we were to water. We'd known one another for some time, were familiar with each other's lives and work, and both served on the board of the same nonprofit organization. The nonprofit's retreat was the reason we were in town. Truthfully, I was also there specifically to meet Austin in person, this woman I admired, to see for myself if she might become as special to me as I suspected.

By the time we left the retreat, I was certain. I called my husband, Kelly, on the car ride home. I wanted to check in with him about my time away and I also wanted to tell him about this person I'd just met. I told him, "I love her.' He said he could hear my smile over the phone as I described how much I enjoyed spending time with Austin, how talking with her felt like making more than a friend. It felt like finding a sister.

I'll be honest. That kind of lightning-quick connection is a rare occurrence for me, and I was exhilarated. What's more, I was inspired.

During our beachside chat, Austin shared an idea she had for a book. She'd already been working on it for some time but felt a little stuck in her process toward completion. I could relate, as I was in the same place with my own work in progress. In its current state, her book was still too amorphous, too unruly. But even as I listened to her wrestle with the idea, and work out how to contain it, I saw her eyes brighten with a new concept mid-speech. What if the work resisted restraint because it was not meant to be restrained? What if she had very nearly everything she needed for the book to take shape, except for the courage to let it find its own shape? She stopped wrestling with the work so she could dance with it instead.

I watched the wheels turn right in front of me, and I saw in Austin a mind simultaneously at work and play. I saw a writer doing their job and a woman remembering who the hell she was and what she wanted.

I know now, after reading *Full of Myself*, how she became that woman sitting before me and I hold an even greater respect for the strength it took to so thoroughly reclaim her own voice. Now I know, after reading it, why her voice resounds. I know why her laugh is contagious. I know why she chose to share her pain, her love, her wisdom in these pages.

To me there is nothing more progressive than a Black woman who decides to include herself in her desire to save the world. It doesn't matter how long it takes to get there. How could it, in a world that continues to fight for the right to silence and dismiss us? The fact that Austin held on to herself is miraculous, and a damn good story. In the following pages, we all receive the gift of her maintaining the spark I saw in her eyes two years ago. Keep reading. She'll tell you all about it.

With love,
Ashley C. Ford

Introduction

THE ONLY THING worse than being fired is being asked to fire yourself. It's so lukewarm. Your supervisors don't feel strongly enough to terminate you outright and offer a severance package. Instead—at least in my case—they resort to a polished mean girl policy, revealing that you're unwanted, but you're welcome to stick it out if your health benefits are really that important. I'll never forget being called into that meeting with my supervisors.

I've worked at this predominately white megachurch for two years. I typically meet with my bosses separately because I have two roles: event planner and DEI coordinator. But they've called a meeting today with the three of us to "learn how to better support me."

My coworker walks into my office and finds me on my hands and knees, sprawling across huge sheets of easel pad paper. With a blue marker, I'm listing my various job duties. "Whoa," she responds to the mess. "What's all this?"

"My job," I respond, before telling her about the meeting I'm preparing for. If my supervisors are willing to offer me more support, I want to make sure they know everything I'm juggling. I finish up just in time to walk over to the meeting. I leave the papers where they are. I don't need them. The floor is in disarray, but my mind is clear.

We do our usual greetings: "How are you?" "How has your day been?" But then it's time to get down to business. The one on my right talks first. "We want to do a better job of supporting you in this work, and we thought it might be helpful to review what we've observed."

"All right," I respond tentatively, still rehearsing my notes.

The one on my left starts talking. "So I'm just going to jump right in. You are responsible for volunteer name tags, but you seem so miserable when you have to print them." That's true. When I went back to school for my master's degree, I didn't picture myself alone in a basement fighting three printers, hoping one of them would willingly print front and back on cardstock.

"I know it wasn't part of your job description," the one on the right adds, "but sometimes you forget to grab the mail and bring it around to everyone." Also true. I already had two roles, but then our office administrator left. Instead of hiring someone new, y'all expected me to take on the duties no one else wanted.

I nod, but my stomach tightens. I'm pretty sure I've been tricked into this meeting. I don't know what this is about, but it's not about offering me support.

"You never got that trip off the ground to visit civil rights museums," continues the one on the right. "And that was one of the reasons you were hired." I stop nodding my head. The two biggest obstacles to that trip are sitting in front of me. I spent months trying to plan it. The one on the left wouldn't give me a budget or a credit card to make reservations. The one on the right wouldn't clear her schedule for dates, with the added stipulation that it was mandatory she attend.

Humiliation and defiance battle in my body. It's true that I haven't been a perfect employee. I do hate fighting with the copy machines. I do sometimes forget that it's now my duty to scour the mailroom on behalf of my team. But I've also given my all to this place.

I've created programs from scratch that no one else could teach. I've brought together multigenerational classrooms where teenagers and boomers are learning together. My classes are growing instead of declining week to week. Every time they've gone back on a promise, I've still found a way forward. Even when the job left me exhausted, frustrated, and scared, I did it because I believed in the importance of the mission: making vague concepts of racial justice real for our community. None of that seems to matter.

I'm trying to keep my breathing even, but what I want to do is gulp for air. They've made a naughty list, it dawns on me. For them, this list is evidence of my incompetence. For me, it's evidence of their betrayals.

Evidence of being ignored.

Evidence of being lied to and scapegoated.

Evidence of being misled and misunderstood.

They continue. I am desperate for something to stop the onslaught—a phone ringing, a knock on the door. Part of me wants to raise my voice, to laugh derisively, to tell them all about themselves. Except I know. I know this isn't a real conversation. There are a few things I've learned in my two years here, and one of them is that decisions are never made in the room. Decisions are made in secret white people meetings-before-the-meeting.

After forty minutes of criticism, the one on my left has a final example. "And we are unsure about the trainings you lead. I received a report from Jane that she walked by an evening training a few weeks ago, and it had gone significantly overtime."

I feel both of my eyebrows raise. A surge of laughter begins in my chest, but I squelch it before it escapes. I finally understand what's happening.

This isn't about my performance at all. This is about wanting me gone so they can hire a volunteer, family member, or friend. The newest darling they've fallen in love with. Someone who's a better "culture fit." They aren't assessing my work, they're building a case. And I know it because there are only two things in the world I'm good at, and one of them is speaking.

I recall the exact training she mentioned. It ran long because the volunteers had so many questions about caring for the poor and assessing their own privilege that they asked if we could stay longer. They gave me a standing ovation at the end. (A little awkward in a room of less than fifty people, but I'll take it!) No, this was not about my job performance, good or bad. This was about letting me go.

"So, with that said," one of them concludes, "we would like to ask if you believe God is still calling you to work here." I'm rendered speechless by her invocation of the Divine.

The other one jumps in. "You know we have a team retreat in two weeks. How about you spend the next couple of weeks wrapping things up, and then you won't have to attend the retreat? You can begin figuring out what's next for you."

They want to disappear me. For the first time in forty minutes, they pause so I can respond.

I don't speak right away. I'm taking in their faces—their true faces—and in that moment I am no longer afraid. I have no desire to advocate to remain at this workplace. I want nothing to do with either of them. I've seen enough. But I'm calculating what is important to me: my husband, my finances, my dignity, my ability to tell my own story. And then I know what to say.

"I had not considered any of this. And I am not prepared to be without a paycheck in the next two weeks. I need time to give all of this some thought, and I'd like to discuss it with my husband before I offer a substantial response."

I stand up and head to my office. I grab my phone from

my purse, holding shame at bay as I press my husband's name. When I hear his voice, all that comes out is a sob. "What's wrong, babe?" he asks.

I feel woozy. And sad. And angry. "I've just been fired," I answer through tears.

Woozy, sad, and angry is how I begin to find myself again.

. . .

POET NAYYIRAH WAHEED writes in her book *nejma:*

> all the women.
> in me.
> are tired.

It's true. Black women are tired. I am tired.

The truth is, I enjoy my work as a racial justice educator. I enjoy talking about antiracism, the multiracial pursuit of justice, the legacy of the Revolution, and the future we could all inherit if we actually valued Black people. I love inspiring those who are new to racial justice, and I love affirming the people who worked tirelessly for equality long before the term "woke" started trending. I love my work. And I am tired.

It's work, being a Black woman in America. We are the backbone of most progressive social movements but ignored when it's time to choose leaders. We are celebrated as the "saviors of democracy" in every election cycle but receive the fewest benefits for doing so. We are the movers and shakers of pop culture but rarely reap the payment we deserve for our brilliance. We are the pillars of our spiritual communities but often battle feeling misunderstood, overwhelmed, and isolated.

In my previous book, *I'm Still Here,* I recounted the difficulties of being outspoken about race in America. I chronicled the awkward interactions with white people and the painful realizations that this world—this white supremacist, imperialist, capitalist, patriarchal world—was not made for our survival. What I am still endeavoring to name in this book is something subtler, something I experienced before being fired from that job: the emotional and physical posture Black women are expected to adopt as we move through the world. In its most simple terms, I call this posture "an emptying." It wants us, Black women, to be emptied of ourselves.

This is an experience far vaguer than the systems we can point to with data—statistics like gender pay gaps and rates of maternal mortality—but I believe many of us have been experiencing this expectation since we were children. Accused of being disrespectful for asking too many questions. Charged with disruption for the same youthful behavior of our peers. Called exclusionary when we sat at the Black kids' table in the cafeteria. Punished for being too loud. I am left wondering if what the world has wanted from us since we were young is to be dispossessed of ourselves—to need nothing, to want nothing, to be nothing, except malleable tools in an antiblack system of exploitation. I bet, even now as an adult, you experience it daily: the expectation that you will trade your truest self for a hollow version that allows white folks to feel more comfortable, more powerful than they already are.

Now, in 2025, DEI budgets have been decimated. Diversity offices forced to close. Book bans on the rise. Affirmative action is no more. Access to a safe abortion is no longer a national right. And while all of these new realities will hit Black women in a particular way, I would argue that this is also a particular attack on our *work:* our work to erect those budgets, to create those offices, to write those books, to access higher education, and to advocate for the healthcare of us all. As progressives wonder what went wrong in an election in which the first Black woman candidate of a major party was dismissed as a "DEI hire," Black women may feel heartbroken, betrayed, even hopeless, but what we are not is surprised. Our work, our character, our stories, are always up for debate in a country that desires the reestablishment of white dominance.

So, what shall we say to these things? How do we respond when the country seems hell-bent on going back in time?

When I started writing this book, I became inspired by a story about the writer and cultural anthropologist Zora Neale Hurston. Ms. Hurston was a brilliant author—it is said that she wrote her novel *Their Eyes Were Watching God* in just seven weeks. But her penchant for storytelling didn't stop on the page. She was known for rewriting herself, exploring all the facets of her individuality, even when that meant changing the details of her life—like when and where she was born. I like to think of Hurston as one of the original quirky Black girls.

In 1934, she was photographed by Carl Van Vechten, who captured the images of many Harlem Renaissance artists. When Zora reviewed her photos, she wrote back to Vechten, "I love myself when I am laughing and again when I am looking mean and impressive." I adore this response. I love that, somewhere deep within, she gravitated to the images of herself that Black women were not supposed to embrace—not in 1934 and not in 2025.

I think Zora was onto something profound in her declaration. Just as we have a right to vote, just as we have a right to equality, just as we have a right to equal protections before the law, we also have a right to the full range of our own humanity—to our laughter and our sadness, to our failings and our growth, to our quirkiness and our impressiveness, to our pain and our healing. The work of self-possession is the justice work we have been made to undervalue.

Our bodies are more than vessels for improving the world. They deserve to be fully inclusive of our needs, wants, and imaginations. Sure, our personhood might very well be a threat to a society built on the assumption of our subjugation. But even if it weren't, even if our self-possession was not tied to justice work in any way, we would still be worthy of it. Our humanity demands it.

We are punished when we laugh too loud, but I love myself when I am laughing. We are punished for failing and again for looking mean and impressive. But I am learning to love myself when I fail to meet the expectations of whiteness. I love myself again when I am looking mean and impressive, even if that makes others uncomfortable. We are rarely thought to be awkward or sad, but I love myself even then. I love myself when I am embodied, though the world would prefer to treat me like a magical negro. It is expected that we will always be too busy healing everyone else to have the time, space, energy, or money to heal ourselves. But I love myself when I am healing.

In this book, I look back at the defining moments when I decided that all the women within me should be free. During a time when Black women are tired—tired of protesting, tired of "saving democracy," tired of educating and explaining—I am interested in what the freedom of self-possession can offer us. I learned at a young age that being "full of myself" was a bad thing. But I have decided that I want to be full of myself: my ideas, my opinions, my curiosities, my needs, my emotions, my self. I want to consider what I'm owed, not only as a citizen but as a human being. And though I suspect there is a certain tired that always comes with the pursuit of justice, I wonder if we'll be just a little less so as we practice valuing our own humanity as much as we care for the humanity of others.

My hope is that you will find within these stories the deep truth of our humanity as Black women, a complexity, a constellation of realities. A humanity to be celebrated. A humanity to be embraced. A humanity that exists not to save the world but to save ourselves. This book is an exploration of hope and joy, of pleasure and grief, of community and autonomy. It's about the complexity of being human and deciding to live.

I Love Myself When
I Am Laughing

Honey, let me tell you that I
LOVE the laughing sound

I love to make the
laughing sound

—ELOISE GREENFIELD,
"HONEY, I LOVE"

Squeals

UNDER THE SUN, we are free. Free from our desks. Free from our chairs. Free from the walls with all the rules. Out here we scream and shout. We pump our legs to leap off swings. We flip over the crossbar before flying down the slide backwards. We pluck dandelions from the grass and fashion them into crowns as our fingertips turn yellow and green. We play tag or kick balls or jump rope until we smell like outside. Even with all this unmitigated frenzy, there are few corners of recess more alive than where the Black girls gather to play hand-clapping games.

First, I watch. My friends at my momma's house sing it different than here at school. But after one round, I got it. I face Joy, staring into her large eyes, effortlessly sliding my hands between hers, and then we are popping our fingers in succession. When we finish, Tiffani shouts, "Y'all ever do the four-people version?"

Three other girls have, and they form a little box. I stand next to Ty and become her shadow, miming her movements—ratatat right, ratatat left, ratatat up, ratatat down. She peeks at me to make sure I'm following. When I get the triple clap right—Tat-Tat-Tat—she gives me a little tap with her hip. I'm beaming with pride.

Now it's my turn to jump in. I'm opposite Alecia. At first I'm concentrating hard, trying not to mess up. But the rhythm finds my hips and soon I'm giggle-singing along with everyone. I'm late when I go left, but I recover without disrupting the rhythm of the other girls. They all smile by opening their eyes a little wider. *You did it!* their faces cheer. When we finish the final *tweedle leet,* Alecia takes two steps forward, sweeping me into her arms. "Ahhhhh!" a half laugh, half shock bubbles out of me, as I give in to her exuberant hug.

"Oh! I know what we should do next!" Ty proclaims. And once again we are rearranging ourselves, switching partners and slapping our hands together—palms to palms, knuckles to knuckles, hands to hips, feet to concrete.

There is a particular magnanimity that happens when you learn a hand-clapping game with Black girls. If you mess up, everyone squeals and dissolves into laughter. If you get the words wrong because your cousin sings it a different way, everyone squeals and dissolves into laughter. If you barely make it to the end, everyone squeals and dissolves into laughter.

There is no one more patient than a Black girl teaching another Black girl when to turn left and then right, and how many times to clap in between. She goes slowly. She is encouraging. She says, "Here, watch," and then makes sure you're imitating. She adds an "ayyye" into the middle of the song when you've got it. She asks if you're ready to try on your own. She wants to include everyone, so we try it with five girls or six girls, as many as we can. It doesn't really work—except it does, because success is measured by the vibrations of our laughter, and our laughter is seismic.

Next we pair up and play Down, Down Baby, which Nelly hasn't stolen yet. We clap our hands. We stomp our feet. We tip our heads for *ding-dong*. We swirl our hips for *hoooot dog*. It's so damn feminine without any of the sexuality that will soon be assigned to any movement of our bodies.

Before recess is over, we have to play Jig-a-low. Tiffani jumps in the center and does her version of the Hammer. Half of us shout "Ohhhh OhOh OhOh" as she gets into it. When Alecia jumps in the center, she does the Roger Rabbit, her beads swing in her face, emphasizing the beat by clicking half a step behind it. She seems prepared because her eyes are closed. When Stephanie jumps in the center, she tugs Brooke with her and they do the Bump.

My nervousness builds as we make our way around the circle. Soon it will be my turn. My hands are shaking. I think I'm going to do the Cabbage Patch. I hope no one beats me to it. When I hear my name, my heart is pounding wildly. Still, I leap into the center and swing my arms one direction twice, then I pause and swing them the opposite way, slowly, emphasizing the movement. The girls shout, "Okay!" and my day is made. I am breathless when I rush back to my place in the circle. My place in the circle. Where my laugh is free. Where my heart is full.

This is how we learn to delight in our own genius. This

is where we learn to live our secrets out loud. No one on the playground seems to notice our presence here or the lack of our presence on the swings over there. Or perhaps they just don't care. I'll never know, because back then it didn't matter to me at all. All that mattered was us and our unequivocal delight in one another.

This laughter—this pure unadulterated laughter that blooms inside the cultural camaraderie of Black girls—keeps us alive. It doesn't always look like hand-clapping games anymore, but we know it when we feel it. It always feels like this. I wish it could always feel like this.

Hair Store Order of Service

Announcements

A LITTLE BELL rings as I enter the store, announcing my arrival. I am immediately made aware of the items on sale thanks to the pink and green neon-colored, hand-drawn signs dotted around the aisles. The bandannas are two for one, the earrings are 40 percent off, and there's an assortment of rattail combs for a dollar. Everyone who walks through these doors does so with faith that we will find what we need.

Praise and Worship

THE BEST HAIR stores have great music: a mix of R&B, followed by hip-hop, before switching to a gospel tune. The sudden change should be jarring, but it feels right as we absentmindedly hum along. We direct an imaginary choir with one hand while searching the aisles and examining new product lines. I can hardly contain myself when a Tevin Campbell song makes it into the rotation, singing the lyrics quietly but definitely out loud. I'm rarely the only one. We wink at one another as we nail the ad-libs word for word.

Greet Your Neighbor

A SHORT BLACK woman from the Bonnet Ministry is talking loudly on the phone, entertaining us all with a story of *what had happened* last night. We try to hide our chuckles at her comedic timing. We mostly fail. She doesn't mind because we've become her amen corner. Bored children pop out from behind racks of braiding hair while we—mothers, aunties, cousins, sisters, friends—slide along the aisles, all "How you doin?" and "Can I reach around you?" I have never been ignored by the Black women in the hair store. Our communion with one another is sometimes just a smile. Sometimes just a nod. Either way, it's all the encouragement I need to get through the day.

Altar Call

BUT I CAN do more than acknowledge the women around me. I can also turn to my neighbor to ask for help. I have to find the right hair with the right brand and the right texture and length for the style I envision. But most of all, it must be the right color. Sometimes what I need is an exact color match, in which case I have to take a chance and ask sis next to me, "Do this look like a match?" as we try to find the right light for our analysis. Sometimes I'm not looking for an exact match, just the right pop of color. I know I've got it when she says, *"Yes, hair!"* or *"Yes, purple!"* In here our choices are not considered weird or ghetto, unprofessional or outlandish. We see one another and honor our creativity. We find sanctuary with one another.

Sermon

I NEVER KNOW what form the sermon is going to take. The women next to me are often willing to dish advice: *Use this mousse to refreshen the ends of those extensions. This brand handles heat well. This hair will hurt your stylist's fingers. This deep conditioner is great for hydration.* In the middle of simple advice, a whole word could be dropped, "Make sure your coils are as big as your joy, honey!" Blessings have been spoken over me time and time again in the beauty supply store.

But there are also words of warning. If our good sis with the good story is still chatting on the phone, she might have reached the get-your-life-together section, where she repeats what she had to tell the person who got on her one last nerve. The absolute read she is repeating for her friend will have us laughing but also thinking. Or perhaps rethinking what we can do differently in our lives to make sure we never get read like this. At this point we can't stifle our cackling at all. This woman needs a microphone and a contract for a stand-up show.

Offering

WHEN MY ARMS can no longer juggle everything in them without dropping a bottle of shampoo every few steps, I know I need to make my way to the checkout counter. This is the place likely to bring us the most laughs, because here we are just waiting. All decisions have been made, and now we are casually talking as we inch our way to the front of the line.

Amusement ripples through us when the woman at the counter, who already has eight bags of hair, runs to get one more. *Just in case.* "Take your time," we tell her, because we have all been there. When the woman in the middle of the line reaches for a pack of gold cuffs, she tells us her little girl is getting braids with extensions for the first time. We grin with pride as if she is the niece of us all. We are almost doubled over when homegirl, only half finished from taking down her last style, testifies about how much she hated it. We are entertained by the teens trying on wigs that look ridiculous until a random find elicits an "Oh, wait a minute. Why is that one kinda cute, tho?" In the beauty supply store, our laughter over the hair adventures that connect us all reminds us of our larger family, the community to which we belong.

Benediction

AS WE DEPART, the blessings we've accumulated cannot be contained in the heavy black bags carrying our newfound products. We also have each other and the simple benediction given to keep our spirits lifted as we leave: "Have a good day, sis."

Inconvenient

I'M PASSING TIME in CVS, waiting for my son to finish daycare. He hates being picked up early when he could still be playing with his friends. I weave through the aisles until I find the "ethnic" hair care section. It's only a quarter of a row, occupying four shelves of product, but I remember when products for us were nothing but boxes of relaxers along with blue magic, pink lotion, and African hot oil. I don't need anything today, but I always enjoy reading about the promises of growth and hydration.

Another Black woman enters the store. The automatic doors haven't finished closing behind her before she asks the cashier for help finding edge control. I scan the beige shelves, quickly noticing they don't carry any. The young white woman is eager to help. She ushers the Black woman over. I take a large step to my right, giving them some room. But with no label available, the cashier isn't sure what she's looking for. She has no idea what edge control is. "Ummmm," she says, mostly to herself.

She pivots, and instead makes a suggestion. "There are some oils down there." She points to tiny bottles of tea tree, coconut, and castor oil. "Or maybe . . ." She trails off as she bends over, trying to get a better look at all the stickers.

The Black woman smiles and thanks her for her help, letting her off the hook.

When the clerk is out of earshot, I whisper, "Don't do it, sis. Don't use that tea tree for edge control."

She lets out a burst of laughter, and we kiki for a few minutes longer. We trade small talk about our favorite products and the biceps strength required for an upcoming wash day. We are complete strangers but you'd never know we didn't walk into that store together. In this moment we see one another and affirm our needs in a place that fails to meet them.

My joke was simple, but our laughter underscores a complex state of realities: that a product fairly basic to our hair care isn't carried in this store while two aisles are dedicated to products for white folks. That any white woman could have asked us for help finding a product we don't use, and we could probably direct her to it anyway. That perhaps we weren't close enough to the Black side of town for this convenience store to be truly convenient.

I have never walked into any convenience store and found that they don't carry an entire product line for white women. It might not be the specific brand one is looking for, but there will always be shampoo, conditioner, hair spray, hair coloring, and all the various accessories made for the texture of white folks' hair. But I am not guaranteed that same access. I will have to at least consider which side of town I'm on. Currently, I live between two Target stores. The one to the south carries two glorious aisles of hair products for Black women. The one to the north, only a quarter of an aisle. The shelves for the products white folks use are identical. When I consider how big the discrepancies continue to be, I can only laugh.

The first time I told this story online, white women were outraged. They accused me of making fun of a clerk who didn't mean any harm. They went to bat for her, and couldn't understand why I would call out a woman who made such an innocent mistake.

None of these women could comprehend that the white clerk was neither the subject of the story nor the punch line of the joke. The Black woman was the subject. The joke was our own inconvenience in a convenience store. We laughed at the absurdity that we are still being left out. It's a laughter that reminds us that we are human, too. Even though our needs would not be met here, we are still here.

I believe with my whole heart that laughing at the inconvenience of our existence is one way in which we keep ourselves sane.

Becky

"GIRL. GUESS WHAT Becky did today, child," Zakiya says as she walks into my apartment and sets her purse on the nearest chair. The "d" at the end of "child" trails off for what I know is about to be some nonsense.

"Hmm. Which Becky, girl?" I ask, planting myself on the couch, leaning toward her so I don't miss a word. There are three Beckys where I work, so I'm trying to figure out which Becky we're talking about.

"Uh-uh, *just* Becky," she says back to me.

"Ha! Got it." I giggle. "Please continue."

Before Beyoncé let out our secret when she told her man off about Becky with the good hair, most white women seemed oblivious to the fact that we have names for their problematic behavior, names that make us laugh. One of those names became ubiquitous in 2020: Karen. It happened largely because of social media, where Black folks could gather and share inside jokes publicly (much like playing hand-clapping games on the playground). But as more white people realized that our naming of their behavior can carry consequences—from going viral for all the wrong reasons to being fired from your job—they became very interested in our lexicon.

Miss Ann and Mr. Charlie are two names that immediately come to mind as examples. Both have been used to describe arrogant, condescending white women and men since the 1920s at least. We've built on the tradition, becoming ever more creative over the years. In 2018 "BBQ Becky" and "Permit Patty" both went viral, but in our homes we've still got all kinds of names for white people who seem oblivious to their own discriminatory behavior.

For example, you can always count on Chad to be the mediocre white man who is committed to interrupting every woman of color he's ever met for her own learning benefit. And Todd is always going to be the one who takes you out for coffee to make you feel welcomed then steals your idea and pretends he did you a favor by taking all the credit. Janie is "trying her best" to practice inclusion, but let her know she made a mistake and you can count on her lashing out at you. Or crying . . . hard. And if you've bumped into any of these personalities at work, you just hope that you don't end up behind a Karen when you stop at the grocery store, because she will hold the entire line hostage until she receives the time and attention she's owed for the emotional suffering of wanting to return an item she paid for in cash and no longer has the receipt.

I can't remember what "Becky" had done to Zakiya that day. But I can promise that we laughed and laughed at whatever unhinged behavior Becky decided to exhibit only because she could. And in the folds of our laughter, we found pockets of comfort. Through our laughter, we con-

firm that we are not overreacting to the dehumanizing behavior we experience so frequently.

Our laughter is a reminder of who *they* become under
the influence of uninterrogated whiteness. Messy. Illogical.
Biased. Malicious. Bigoted. Whiteness really believes the
world belongs only to it, never to us . . . all of us. And in its
destruction of the humanity of others, white folks begin to
lose their own. That is no laughing matter, but naming it is
a relief.

Brutal

MY FATHER-IN-LAW HAS lived in Detroit for the last forty years, but he was born and raised in a small southern town outside Birmingham, Alabama. He became a teenager in the 1960s, when civil rights protests were raging against the system, and the system raged back. After the signs came down and Black folks had the freedom of movement—to sit in any seat, choose any line, and occupy any space—he was ready to take that freedom and run as far and as fast as he could. But he was being raised by a grandmother who was distrustful of this nascent freedom.

My father-in-law often tells the story of going to the bank with his grandmother in the early seventies. He is protective of her and wants to make sure no one takes advantage of her.

"When she got to the front of the line," he says, "there was a young white woman in her twenties who asked if she could help us. So my grandmother tells this young woman what she needs, but every other word is 'ma'am.' To this young girl, you know? She's like 'Thank you, ma'am.' 'Please, ma'am.' 'Yes, ma'am.'"

We can see his frustration building from the memory.

"By the tenth time, I can't take it no more. I lean over and whisper loudly, 'You ain't got to keep calling her ma'am. She should be calling *you* ma'am.' "

He continues, "Do you know she just waved me off, telling me to hush!" His face animates with shock as if this happened yesterday.

He keeps going, telling us that eventually he had to walk out of the bank because she wouldn't stop, and he was livid. That's when we begin to laugh, and someone shouts, "So what you're saying is, you have always been this way?"

When I get upset, my face goes absolutely flat: no emotion, no reaction, no nothing. I am stone. But my father-in-law is the exact opposite. He cannot hide his anger. His face crinkles up like a wad of paper, eyes squinty, nose wrinkled, lips poked out. He makes his angry face as he continues the story, but this is where he gets creative.

In some tellings, his lips were poked out so far, "they dragged on the floor" as he left. Or they were poked out so far that they reached the car door before he did. Or if he makes it into the car, his lips were "poked out far enough to touch the windshield." We all giggle, shaking our heads at his illustration.

He is easy to rile up, which feels completely at odds with his otherwise quiet, easygoing demeanor. He is not loud or overbearing or entitled. But he often thinks humans are ridiculous, and his tolerance for us all can be quite low. And so he laughs at himself as he tells the story, and we laugh imagining it.

At the end, he tells us that he couldn't even sit still in the car. He had to get out. "I slid out of my seat, took a quick look around, and slammed that car door back as hard as I could," he tells us. "I think I shook the whole block."

"Why did you look around before slamming the door?" we ask, setting him up for his punch line.

"Because the white folks might have been watching."

There he sits, pretending to be dumbfounded by our burst of laughter at the irony. He keeps his face deadpan as long as he can before our laughter becomes contagious and his body forces him to chuckle, too.

I love this story. I love all his stories about growing up Black and southern, but the story isn't actually funny. I mean not *really*. Because we all know why his grandmother couldn't break her habit. We all know she wasn't trying to rile up her grandson. She wasn't teasing him or purposefully pushing his buttons. She was doing what had become rote, what life had taught her was necessary in order to keep herself and her family safe. And, even though my father-in-law wanted to embrace the protections of his civil rights, he knew he needed to look around first. He was not all the way free either. Not yet. And so we laughed.

I am convinced this is how some of our most brutal stories survive, even if they aren't actually funny. They survive because ensconced in laughter is the only way our bodies can bear them. The poet and artist Morgan Harper Nichols says that if we had to re-feel the weight of the trauma within our stories, many of them would remain buried, never to be passed on. But our ability to focus on personality or a weird quirk or a turn of phrase—anything to make us all laugh—means the story gets to live on.

Stickers

NOT ALL OF our laughter holds space for our trauma, of course. My toddler comes home with a sticker. He is so excited to show me, he follows me into the bathroom. I squeal in excitement as he lifts it toward my face.

I bend over to ask, "Did you get that for being so good today?"

He looks off to his left as if the answer is standing nearby, then looks down at the sticker in the center of his tiny palm.

"Hmm," he says as his eyes find mine. "Not really." He shrugs before clutching his sticker again and racing out of the room.

I laugh hard, giving in completely to my delight in him.

And I wish. I wish I could give all Black children, all Black people everywhere a sticker, even if they weren't *really* so good today.

I Love Myself When I Am Failing

Wrong is not my name

—JUNE JORDAN,
"POEM ABOUT
MY RIGHTS"

Off Beat

SEVEN THOUSAND EMPTY chairs stare back at me from the stage of the megachurch. I'm in my mid-twenties, a year and a half into working here, but much of this world still feels inscrutable to me. Everything is immense. They have a lexicon to describe small churches like the one I grew up in: words like "stripped down" and "organic." This place does not do stripped down or organic. Here, everything is extravagant and structured. That's why I'm onstage on a Thursday afternoon.

We are rehearsing for the three services that will take place over the weekend. My only job is to read a few Bible verses while the piano plays underneath my voice. *Easy*, I think to myself. Even though this is my first time doing so at this church, I've spoken in services since I was fourteen years old, brandishing a microphone, reciting Bible verses from memory with a choir of thunderous voices behind me. Truth is, I prefer talking to thousands of strangers from a stage over sitting one-on-one with an acquaintance while sipping coffee. But I've only just stepped onto this stage, and it already feels foreign.

Blue floodlights turn on, and a yellow spotlight strikes me. Darkness swallows all seven thousand seats. All I can make out are the shadows of two white men directing me from the second row. A piano player sits onstage behind me, his fingers dancing out an emotional tune that begins gently, then gradually builds, expanding itself inside our chests.

One of the men signals for me to begin. I read in time to the music, my voice starting soft before rising and falling with the swells of the piano. As the song builds, my voice grows deeper and more urgent. They stop me midsentence. I fold my hand across my eyebrows in an attempt to view the person talking. It doesn't really work.

"Austin, could you read it faster?" one of the voices asks.

"Sure," I respond, confidently beginning again. This time I increase my tempo. I adjust my cadence to give it more life, more intensity right from the start. The energy in my body follows my recitation. Though the movement is imperceptible to those watching, I'm keeping time inside.

The same voice stops me again, asking me to change up once more. I don't mind. I understand that different rhythms will have different impacts on those listening. Cadence makes a world of difference in the Black church, too. I am willing to try as many times as needed until they sense the music and I are in harmony for the mood they hope to create in the room. I try again.

One of the men walks closer to the stage. I can actually see his face now. He waves his arm, signaling me to stop again. "Actually, Austin, could you just ignore the music?

We don't want you to read in time to the song at all. Just pretend you don't hear it."

I am stunned. Completely bewildered. I hear myself offering a high-pitched "Sure!" and for a moment, I can't figure out who just spoke on my behalf. The voice turns inward. *Chile, I don't know what these people want, but you can read, so start reading.*

I try, but my internal pulse doesn't have an off switch. I plant my feet in an attempt to prevent my body from rocking to the rhythm of the music. I'm standing perfectly still, but this feels unnatural, too. Not only is my body used to moving to the sound of music, but it is used to moving when I'm onstage. I walk. I gesture. I point. I look at every corner of the room. Usually my whole body is an active participant, but now I can't trust her. I struggle to make my body heavy, like cement. But it has no desire to be hardened. It wants to respond to the melody it hears, to the words I'm reading, to the moment when every seat will be filled and someone may be hanging on to this passage for dear life. I'm yelling at all my individual body parts: *Legs, stop that. Hips, you can't do that right now. Arms, you are focused on holding this Bible, okay? Don't do nothin' else.* Great. Now I sound like my momma giving me instructions not to touch anything in the store. Is any of this working?

Halfway through the selection, I have no idea what I've just read. I'm completely in my head. For such a long time, I figured many white people just lacked rhythm. It never occurred to me they might be purposefully ignoring their inner groove. Why? Why would you do that?

I consider taking the advice of the shadowed man. Could I pretend the music isn't playing at all? How would I read this in a silent room? It doesn't take long to discover that my voice will create its own rhythm. Even without music, there is a pulse that propels the notes in my voice box. There is a gentle beginning, and then a gradual rising that I hope will unfold itself inside those listening. Every pause matters. Every question and every declaration has its own progression. Even when I'm reading without music, there is a harmonious presence that invites me to be in tune with every body. But in this moment, I am utterly disconnected from myself. I am a bundle of realizations, and none of them helpful in giving these men what they want.

I don't know how to assess if I'm doing well or failing miserably. Does the worse it sounds to my ear mean it's getting better? A single drop of sweat slides down my right side. My body is hot from all the energy I'm expending to force myself to be still. I imagine the lights illuminate my growing discomfort, and for the first time in my life, I'm desperate to exit stage left. Usually gracing the stage is a euphoric, out-of-body experience for me, but not today. Today I am in my body but demanding that it perform like someone else's.

There were meetings after this rehearsal, and again after the services concluded. A pronouncement was given on how I did. I don't remember if it was good or bad. (Although this was the last time I was asked to be onstage, so maybe that's a clue.) Nonetheless, for perhaps the first time at this job, I did not care to know if anyone thought I did well. Under those watchful eyes, it dawned on me that my best would never be good enough. My best was not what they were looking for. They were looking for *their* best wrapped in my body. Their definition of good. Their definition of right. Their definition of leadership. I could see it so clearly, and had no desire to reach it.

I did not want to be rhythmless. I did not want to be discordant. I did not want to sacrifice the gift of cadence given to me by the Black folks who raised me. I did not want to exchange my truth for theirs. It was a standard that was beneath me.

I failed at being them. It was a failure I was proud of, because I did not fail at being me.

Power

MY POSITION AT this job is split. Part of my duties are events planning, while my other duties fall under the category of diversity work. It has taken me months to gain approvals for the proposal of a new DEI initiative, even though this initiative is why I've been hired. I'm having trouble figuring out what the leadership actually wants. I wonder if they know what they actually want. I remember placing a newly edited proposal in front of my supervisor. With a sweeping gesture she strikes the language in one sentence and writes something new. I make the changes and bring it back to her the following week, where she takes issue with the exact phrase she added, forgetting it was hers.

It's been a frustrating experience. I care deeply about the language used to describe diversity efforts, and I do want to ensure that everyone is on the same page. And yet, this nitpicking doesn't feel productive. We aren't prioritizing learning, discussing activities, or outlining the curriculum. We are just changing the word "unity" to "amalgamation" and back again. I never leave a meeting feeling that we are making progress toward clarifying a shared vision. We seem to be stuck in an endless loop of quibbling over inconsequential synonyms for this document.

After weeks of trying, when I have managed to piece together acceptable words for the proposal, I must meet with several members of the executive team to sell it. One by one, approvals are given until there is only one meeting left. I need permission from the top, our CEO.

For this meeting, four of us are seated at a mahogany conference table: myself, my supervisor, the CEO, and my partner in trying to pull this off, Jenny. She and I sit directly across from one another so we can read each other's faces.

Each of us has a paper copy of the one-page proposal in front of us. If we receive the okay, Jenny, my small team of volunteers, and I can start advertising our new class on racial justice.

The meeting is quick. The CEO reviews the proposal in less than ten minutes.

"This looks good," he says.

Except for one thing.

"Austin, can I borrow your pen?" he asks. Without waiting for my response, he picks it up and draws an x over one word: "power." Then he flips the paper around so we can all view his change.

"I don't want discussions about power," he says, turning toward me. "You start talking about power and things get messy quickly."

I look at Jenny. Jenny looks at me. Of course. That's what this series of meandering meetings has been all about. Power. And who has it.

And making it clear that I do not.

Radicalized

THE REAL TROUBLE at this job was set in motion thousands of miles beyond its walls. It started when Sybrina Fulton stood on a rally stage in Florida and made the nation aware of the murder of her son Trayvon Martin. He went to the corner store for a snack. He was assumed to be a criminal by a fellow citizen. He was followed. He was attacked. He fought back. For that, he was shot and killed. We waited for months to see if Florida's Stand Your Ground Law would actually apply to this Black boy or if it would be used to justify his murder.

My husband and I had read about the Stand Your Ground Law. Like many Black people, we'd discussed its potential for being used against us, to justify the murder of Black folks. Trayvon's case is the exact scenario we played through our minds.

We learn more and more details as the story gains traction in media outlets. Outrage unfurls when President Obama remarks that if he had a son, he'd look like Trayvon. That's how I felt when I saw Trayvon's photo, like he was mine. There is a familiarity in Trayvon's photographs. An unnamed glimmer that Black people recognize—the hint of sweetness we still see in our boys as they are becoming men but aren't there yet. There is a hopefulness, an innocence that their growing awareness about the world has not yet destroyed. There is an imperceptible babyness that remains even after the physical evidence has melted away—a certain light in the corners of their eyes, a certain ease in their smiles, a certain sound in their laughter, a certain crack in their suddenly deep voices. Black boys are not frightening strangers to us. In this way, Trayvon feels like he is all of us and everyone we love.

Even after all these years, I struggle to explain exactly why his murder dug into my bones. I think it might be because it was my worst fear for my little brother. For most of his childhood, I was his protector, and I took that job very seriously. Granted, I believed it was my right to exercise big sister punishments when he ripped the heads off my Barbies or stuffed a cookie down the throat of my Baby Alive doll or broke my Teddy Ruxpin cassette player . . . but from outside forces, it was my job to protect him.

I have a vague memory of a kid picking on my little brother when he was six. It was after school. Students from every grade were stuffed into the gymnasium, waiting for our parents to get off work at 5:00 P.M. Eric ran up, telling me a kid was making fun of him. Fury rose into my chest. "Who?" I said, following him through a mass of kids, ready to light someone on fire. When Eric stopped in front of the offender, I discovered he was much smaller than me, and I would not in fact have to light anything on fire. Still, I got close, taking full advantage of the height difference, and declared, "This is my brother. Whatever you're doing, stop. Got it?" I don't think I even waited for a response. I just turned to my brother and asked, "You okay?" and that was that.

But within a few years, my brother will have grown to my height. And by the time he is in junior high, he towers over me. I can't protect him anymore. I can't stop anyone who assumes the thirteen-year-old standing before them isn't actually seventeen. When he starts driving, I can't stop police officers from pulling him over. I can't stop school counselors from telling him that his college goals are too lofty for a Black boy. When he lands his first job, I can't follow him around and assure strangers they have nothing to fear. I can't stop people from calling him "articulate." I can't protect him from their utter shock that he is funny and generous and kind and one of the smartest people they'll ever meet.

So, when I heard about Trayvon Martin, and saw his photo, and read about his hoodie, and thought about him walking alone, scared because he was being followed . . . it broke my unspoken fears wide open.

And I was hurt that this child I never met was gone.

It felt deeply personal.

And it always will.

When all was said and done and Trayvon's aggressor was acquitted, I was furious if not surprised. And I wasn't alone. Our church staff heard the news on Saturday night, and on Sunday morning the Black folks (and our allies) at this predominately white church arrived ready. We were ready to alter the order of service. We were ready to speak. We were ready to replace the songs. We were ready to re-write the sermon. We were ready to change everything.

We desperately wanted to speak, to share our pain and frustration with a community that claimed to love us, claimed a commitment to racial justice. Instead, we were told that nothing would change. The original plan for the service would remain, as if nothing had happened, as if our hearts had not been turned inside out. The disappointment was thick.

By the end of the service, the only person who had used their power and influence to speak to our pain was the guest speaker for that day. She did so in defiance of a direct order not to. She changed her sermon. She acknowledged our pain. She gave us hope. Her conviction stood in stark opposition to the silence of our own leadership.

When the service was over, I walked backstage into the green room. To my surprise, it was filled with Black folks. Vocalists, musicians, and staff members who gave hours upon hours to the church had called a meeting. Allies who wanted to be in solidarity with them dotted the room. The tension was unmistakable as I skirted the room, finding an empty spot against the wall. In the center of the room, the pastor sat with elbows on his knees, his hands on either side of his head declaring his apologies. His voice shook as he explained how sorry he was that fear had kept him from speaking. "I just feel like I have disappointed all of you."

He pleaded for understanding as he turned red with emotion, his white hair flopping into his eyes.

No one responded. No one said *It's okay* or *We know your heart*, or offered any relief from the discomfort. In that brief moment of silence, I knew I was going to be fired.

No one is allowed to make rich, powerful, white men feel bad about themselves and their decisions. I was definitely going to lose my job, not because I had done anything wrong that weekend; I don't think I spoke one word that day. But my diversity and inclusion work at the church had raised expectations of the pastor and the leadership staff. Rather than his stepping up in this moment and showing how important our emotional lives were, we were once again sacrificed on the altar of white comfort. Fear that white people would be uncomfortable or even angry at the mention of the case was more important than our heartbreak.

I had been teaching and leading workshops in which I did not define the word "power," as instructed. Nonetheless, everyone recognized the power holder . . . and it was not me. I could not singlehandedly represent the church's commitment to racial justice. And I wouldn't shield the leadership team from the people who were expecting more. As the closest thing to a DEI officer that we possessed, I was supposed to endorse the system. I was supposed to use my Blackness to protect the good white people against any accusations of hypocrisy. I was supposed to calm everyone down. I was supposed to let the pastor off the hook. I was supposed to offer grace. Whatever power I had been handed was supposed to be used in service of their own. And I failed at that job, purposefully.

Just a few weeks later, I was asked to fire myself.

Fired

AS MY SUPERVISORS tell me why they believe I should walk away from my job, a jumble of emotions swirl through my body. But the one I feel persistently in the days after is *tired*. I am so damn tired of repeating the same pattern over and over again. Regardless of my position, my tenure, or my salary, I cannot escape the expectation that the only line of my job description that truly matters is "other duties as assigned." I will be expected to act as a one-woman caterer during an after-hours event. I will be asked to stock the bathrooms with toilet paper and paper towels when the custodian has left for the day. I am expected to make the space, to serve my team, to do so with a smile.

In short, in almost every job I've possessed I have been subject to what I'm calling "legally sanctioned white-collar wage theft," and every Black woman I know has been subject to it at some point in her career. That one little clause, "other duties as assigned," becomes the contractual obligation to say yes to everything without ever expecting additional compensation or support for the extra workload, time, and energy.

I had sat in that office, and others like it, being chided because I couldn't perfectly perform the three jobs I was actually responsible for, and that failure was contributing to my warped sense of self. Everything I thought I knew about myself as a good worker, dependable, likable, felt suspect. In meetings after meetings, I said nothing about my accomplishments, nothing about my workload, nothing about the ways I had been let down. Because I had agreed to their rules.

And I was slowly losing myself.

Sometime between standing on that stage and sitting in this meeting, I realized there were numerous areas in which I was trying to work out of rhythm with myself. I was out of rhythm when I heard my voice go up five octaves to show my excitement at having to work after hours . . . again. I felt out of rhythm when I automatically laughed at a reference I didn't even understand. Every day I resisted my standards being rearranged—independence valued over collaboration, power hoarding celebrated over power sharing, loyalty mattering more than morality, and I was supposed to be grateful for this rearrangement. Maintaining my own standards left me out of rhythm with the organization, and it was making me bone-weary tired.

This realization did not make being fired any easier. But it did help me determine what I had to do next for myself.

The Interview

I WAS A mess . . . for a little while. But my heart healed, and it turned out the church's letting me go taught me a terrible lesson because once I knew that I could survive, no one could threaten me with being fired ever again. By the time job prospects started calling me back to schedule interviews, my posture was completely different than it had been in any interview process I'd entered before.

My father always told me that during an interview I'm not the only one being interviewed; the representatives of the organization are also being interviewed, by me. But it never really felt that way. Even when I did ask questions of the organization, they were designed to make me sound thoughtful or interesting. I never asked questions I truly wanted answers to. They held the job, and I needed the job.

After being let go, I can no longer ignore my own wants and needs when it comes to a healthy workplace. I have no desire to repeat all the awkward, demeaning, dismissive encounters I have had in the past while I desperately hold on to my health benefits. I need a job, but I need one that won't slowly kill me.

The full-time job I am most interested in is becoming one of the resident directors at a college. I show up for the interview, and things are going well. I am interviewed by multiple departments and given a tour of the campus. When I start my panel interview with the residence life department, where my position will be located, a significant portion of the questions are situational: *What would you do if one student froze another student's underwear? What would you do if two roommates got into a fistfight? What would you do if students put a frog in the community bathroom?* The purpose is to assess whether I have the fortitude, creativity, and sometimes sense of humor required for working with college students. But I don't answer right away when they ask, "What would you do if a group of drunk student athletes are being disruptive outside the dormitories at 3:00 A.M.?"

I know the answer I'm supposed to give. I am supposed to say, "I would march outside, authoritatively instruct them to quiet down, collect their IDs, make sure no one is in danger of passing out, and follow the school's protocols for handling inebriated students."

But I know that is not, in fact, what I would do. I hesitate. I'm deciding if I'm going to give the answer I should, or risk losing the job right now by forcing them to deal with all of me.

I'm too tired to work for another employer that wants to pretend they can't see me until it's MLK Day and they momentarily need me to be a Black woman. I have already learned that I cannot be likable enough for whiteness; likability is impossible when it's predicated on being just like them. I will never be just like them.

I take a deep breath and give my honest answer. "I am a Black woman who is the same size as most of these students, and it is entirely possible that a predominately white student body won't always recognize my authority in broad daylight, let alone at 3:00 A.M. while drunk. If these are male athletes, I'd like to be able to tell you that I would immediately confront them, but that doesn't feel safe to me. What I would actually do is contact campus security and have them meet me. I would explain the situation to them, and together we would confront the students. I am happy to take the lead, but it's important to me in this circumstance to have a presence that students will immediately recognize as authoritative at three o'clock in the morning. I would quiet them down, ensure everyone is safe, and follow our protocols." With that, I stop talking. No additional caveats. No softening my language. I just let the answer stand.

This is the moment when I am interviewing them. I've never felt like this before. In every other interview I've had I made references to movies I haven't watched and books I haven't read. I've nodded like I believe the diversity statements and am impressed by all the "work" they've done to be more inclusive. I have asked questions I already know the answers to—questions intended to make me look smart and engaged and to prove I read the website. Until this moment, I have never asked an organization a question that could make or break whether I say yes to them.

But I cannot do it anymore. I can't walk into one more organization where I pretend that I'm not an absolute gift to them. I can't walk into one more workplace that expects to gain from my presence but doesn't want to deal with my realities. I am no one's site for excavation. I cannot allow white supervisors who are incapable of adequately assessing their own mediocrity to be in charge of assessing my gifts or my needs. I would rather not get the job than have to pretend to be just like them another day in my life. If they take me out of the running for needing something different than my white coworkers do . . . if they punish me for wanting to protect myself from racism and sexism . . . then I know this is not the job for me.

I wait for their reactions. I am prepared for them to gently chide me by saying they are looking for someone willing to handle the situation independently. I am prepared for their reassurances that the student body is full of wonderful kids who would never disrespect me just because I'm a Black woman. Either of these responses will be the wrong one. If they give me one of these answers, I will remain polite. I will also take myself out of the running for this position.

Instead, they nod and respond, "We understand," before moving on to the next scenario. And that's when I have faith, that just maybe this time, this department, this team will let me be . . . me.

They offered me the job, and I took it.

Refusal

I CAN ONLY imagine how much of a headache I caused my supervisor after they hired me. Because making me feel safe meant inviting me to make more requests, more than I ever considered voicing before.

I don't know if it's well-documented, but I can tell you from personal experience that white people love to host retreats in the boonies. Whether for staff development, recreation, or strategic planning, if white people have an excuse to venture to the middle of nowhere, they will do so with gusto. Now that I'm a leader in the department with my own student staff, I am expected to take my team to the boonies, too, for some team building. But navigating the wilderness isn't a part of my skill set. I have some great-grandparents who lived in the country, and they would have made excellent guides. But the following generations of my family chose city life, so I know nothing about being *outside* outside. I am pretty good at inspiring people, but not so much when I'm scampering away from the insect buzzing by my ear.

So I ask if I can create my own retreat. An urban one . . . with working toilets. I want to show up in the best way possible for my team. I ask my supervisor for permission to teach them about service by setting up volunteer opportunities in the community. Let me take them to neighborhoods where my white students are in the minority so they glimpse what it's like for marginalized students on their floor. Let me take them to the local hip-hop church so they can see that even within Christianity, how they worship isn't how everyone worships. Let me take them to different restaurants so they don't think it's "weird" to eat certain foods. Let me do what I do best. Let me lead them.

And I did. I led my team my way, with the full backing of my supervisor and colleagues.

For the first time, I didn't have to feign gratitude. I was genuinely grateful for my place of employment. It is a strange thing to say that one of the best jobs I had was at a historically Dutch, predominately white, traditionally conservative college. There were plenty of issues on campus and plenty of spaces where I did not feel safe. But within my department, within my team, I felt completely seen and secure. And it changed the way I showed up every day.

This job did not ask me for a proposal or launch into a stupefying approval process before allowing me to incorporate racial justice work into my job. They welcomed my creativity with open arms.

I was far more honest about my opinions regarding policy and expectations. I was far more adventurous, stepping out of my comfort zone (often into the boonies) because I could tell my team what I needed from them. I was more vocal because I knew I was being listened to—which didn't always mean getting what I wanted, but at least I knew I was heard. Their trust in me gave me room to try out new programming and collaborate on projects that were lifegiving to me. At so many of my previous jobs, I was expected to empty myself; it was here that I first began to become full of myself.

I Love Myself When
I Am Connected

The pieces I am, she gather
them and give them back to
me in all the right order.

—TONI MORRISON,
Beloved

Solidarity

IF IT SOUNDS like I was fired and then immediately grew wings like a phoenix rising from the ashes, know that my story isn't quite that linear. My couch and I became one for days on end as I looked vacantly at the TV and then out the window and then back at the TV. I agonized over every conversation I could remember. I listed and relisted all the critiques of that final meeting. I daydreamed about what I should have said. I woke up every morning next to embarrassment and fell asleep every night next to shame. I was devastated at being fired.

Thankfully my friends didn't let me wallow on that couch for too long. I didn't magically grow wings—my friends became my wings. They helped me ride out the storm of emotions that took place between the moment I was fired and when I found a new place to belong.

My former supervisor had regularly chided me for my propensity to collaborate. In my experience, it is not unusual for white folks to idealize independence—the steel-jawed leader who carries the day on their shoulders even if it almost kills them. It is a difficult expectation for those of us who value collaboration. So many times, my consensus building was viewed as a lack of confidence. Coleading was interpreted as an inability to handle the pressure. And when I asked one question too many in an interdepartmental meeting, I was told by my supervisor to "fake it till you make it, because that's what a leader does." I wasn't incompetent. I was connected. And thank the ancestors, because when I was let go, those connections showed up for me.

When the announcement is made that I will not be at the job much longer, I discover that I am not as isolated as I feel. There are a handful of people who are not willing to accept the narrative that there is no longer room for me.

Some covertly challenge the assertion that there isn't money in the multimillion-dollar budget to continue funding part-time work on DEI matters. Others are overt. Steve tells my supervisor that he is aware of the situation, and that how she treats me will determine whether he stays with the organization. He is a Black man and the most recognized musician onstage; his leaving would be conspicuous to everyone in a way that my leaving will not be.

These interventions from friends buy me time. There are two months' worth of meetings in which I continue to be paid but the only work I'm doing is sitting quietly in a meeting while my colleagues push the organization on its commitments to diversity. I have time to keep receiving a paycheck. I have time to look into my options for other jobs. But mostly they buy me time to see the impact I made. I will not be disappeared. I get to say thank you before I say goodbye.

Rocking

BEFORE THE COLLEGE takes me on, I am rescued by a Black woman. Chi Chi hires me. During my interview with her, it takes every ounce of professionalism I have not to crawl into her lap. When I easily list my faults but struggle to offer an answer for my proudest accomplishments, she invites me to take a deep breath. When her supervisor joins us for a bit and my hands start shaking, she gives me a pen so I have something to hold. When I am self-deprecating, she doesn't join in. She offers me a different viewpoint and invites me to rephrase my imperfections as strengths. Her presence exudes a level of safety I have not experienced in the workplace in a long time. After our interview (where I do refrain from sitting on her lap) she offers me a contractual position doing more diversity work until I can land a full-time job. But more important, she helps me unknot the lies twisting around my heart.

I'll never forget sitting in my first staff meeting. Five of us are gathered to plan an event uplifting the importance of social justice. We are tossing out ideas for a one-day event to show our neighbors in downtown Chicago that our organization cares about the community—from the ones thriving in high-rises to the ones surviving under bridges.

Chi Chi stands at the whiteboard with a red dry-erase marker in her hand, writing down ideas as everyone builds a body of possibilities. I haven't said anything yet, just sit smiling and nodding as other people share. I keep moving in my chair, balancing it on the front two legs. I let my chest fall gently into the table. Then I tense my muscles to control silently setting the chair back onto all four legs. And I do it again and again. This strange rocking of my body is assuaging my anxiety.

I have a suggestion, too, but I just cannot open my mouth to share it. It's been a long time since I've spoken up. I have been punished for saying the wrong thing. I have been re-interpreted when I've said something meaningful. My words have been used against me, thrown back in my face when I least expect it. I have felt completely alienated and unappreciated in meetings for at least a year. I will myself to stay present, but it's hard not to revisit every awful meeting I've endured in the recent past.

"Austin, do you have an idea? You're so quiet over there," Chi Chi says. The table turns to me. I fix my eyes on Chi Chi. I know her the best. I am trying to trust that she won't harm me, even if my idea *is* terrible. I take a deep breath as I lift myself on the front two legs of the chair again. The caveats I offer are a mile longer than the idea itself: "It might not work or it just might not be a good idea, but I did have one little thought that sparked during this conversation . . ." Finally, I offer my one-sentence idea.

"Oh, I like it," she says and writes it on the whiteboard.

The others agree and start adding to it. Then a new idea is thrown out and the conversation moves on. I can hear their voices, but I am entranced by the board.

My body relaxes and my chair lands with a muffled thud onto the soft carpet. My eyes fill with tears as I look at my idea up on the board written in Chi Chi's all caps. It's been so long since anything I've said has made it onto the board. A lump in my throat starts to form as I try to remember: When was the last time anyone said I had a good idea? I'm drawing a complete blank. But there it is now. There is my contribution.

Slowly, purposefully, Chi Chi reminds me of my value— not more important than anyone else, but not less important either. She pulls out of me the knowledge I have accrued, the experiences I have endured, and considers them meaning-ful. She stands with me against the idea that I am inconse-quential. She shows me that I can fight back and reclaim what I know to be true about myself. That I matter.

I am forever grateful to Chi Chi and all the Black women who pulled me back from the edge when I was on the verge of losing myself.

Lost + Found

WHILE I'M WORKING part-time for Chi Chi and applying to full-time jobs in Michigan, I also write.

Blogging is still going strong as a way for those of us who have zero hopes of being invited to write for *Essence* or *The New York Times* to make our voices heard. We cultivate our own little communities online. Some women write honestly about motherhood and marriage. Some women write about travels and singleness. Some women write about media and pop culture. Some women write about theology and spirituality. Some women write about fashion or gaming or politics or food or tech or literature.

Every week for four years, I sit at my laptop and try to make sense out of national racial events. The Obamas are still in office, and a number of people believed his presidency would usher in a postracial era. (Meaning many white folks thought if we elected a Black president, none of us would have to talk about race ever again.) Instead, the Obamas' tenure in the White House is filled with examples of how race remains quite relevant in America. His campaign begins with having his birth certificate challenged, and in his final year in office, he leads us in mourning the loss of Black congregants from the Mother Emanuel church shooting. During this era, I make it my duty to challenge any notions that we have finished our racial justice work as a nation.

Christena is the one who finds me. At the time she is a professor at a predominately white college, like the ones I've attended my entire life. She has a large platform and has written a successful book on diversity. She was the first person I followed on the social media site formerly known as Twitter. She consistently uses her feed to talk about her own experiences navigating predominately white spaces. Her words are a balm to me, affirming my own experiences. She is fierce, and white supremacy doesn't stand a chance when she logs on. She seems so unlike me in her boldness, her willingness to call a white sheet a white sheet. Where I have cultivated the tendency to stew quietly, she teaches me that I can be bold and survive.

One day I would read Audre Lorde and recognize that my silence had not saved me. One day I would read Audre Lorde and tears would stream down my face as I recognized the importance of my own anger. One day I would read Audre Lorde and step into myself. But before Audre, there was Christena. She put her own jobs in jeopardy as she called out injustices, both nationally and at her workplace. She refused speaking engagements if she got a whiff that all they wanted was to put her picture on the website. She refused to align with the darlings who were trending within justice conferences if she believed their teachings were anti-thetical to actual freedom work. She received hate mail and death threats, but still she refused to be silent. She was my little contrarian inspiration who didn't mind tearing down the system, who spoke truth to power, who made decisions in direct opposition to receiving the privileges that come with compliance. She was about that life.

So when she sent me an email that simply said, "Can I feature your essay on my blog?" it meant everything. Everything.

And she did. She shared my writing with her audience and told everyone where to find more. Because of her, I developed a phenomenon called "readers" instead of writing into the void. But more than that, Christena invited me, through her own writing, to take another step into myself, into my body, and to tell my truth.

When I first started writing, I didn't even do it under my own name. My first blog was called *Sankofa Narratives* because I was afraid of how my workplace would respond if they knew the writer was me. My first few posts rarely expressed how racism *feels*, how it sits in my body, how it toys with me. I managed to keep my feelings out of my writing altogether, preferring to treat each post like an unemotional, step-by-step guide. But the more I responded "Hell yes!" to Christena's writing, the braver I felt to tell my own stories.

Once I start revealing my heart, I can't go back. I can't be that kind of silent again. After every post I write, I ask myself one question before hitting the publish button. *Is this true?* And every time I can answer yes—*Yes, it is this painful. Yes, I am this scared. Yes, I am this angry. Yes, racism is this evil*—then I push the button. And the words change me. The words Christena writes. The words I write. They make me braver one sentence at a time.

Open Door

MY BLOG IS growing, and my mentor, Brenda Salter McNeil, has flown to Chicago to have a meeting with her editor. At this point in my life, she is the only Black woman I know who's a full-time writer and speaker. I started working as her assistant at nineteen and quite simply refused to let her go after the job was done. She is back in town to have a conversation about her third book.

I have an obsession with books, but I have never witnessed the inner workings of the publishing industry. So when Brenda invites me to attend the meeting with her, I feel like I've just been invited backstage at a concert.

I pick her up from the airport and drive her downtown for the meeting. We walk into a spacious conference room with windows overlooking the Dan Ryan Expressway as it snakes through the city. I try my best to stay out of the way, but my eyes are wide. *This is amazing,* I keep saying to myself. *This is what a meeting with an editor sounds like.* It's an extraordinary gift to see behind the curtain as they discuss content and timelines. I spend the rest of the day giddy, daydreaming of one day having a publishing meeting of my own.

A week later, the same editor reaches out to me. She has

taken a look at my blog and wonders if I've ever considered submitting a book proposal. I google "book proposals" and start working on one immediately. After having been fired, I want to write a book about what it's like to navigate white spaces as a Black woman and fail . . . miserably. I want to talk about all the little things, the so-called microaggressions, that litter every day and the ways they impacted me. I spend a couple weeks working on the bare bones of it. I don't even have sample chapters; it's just an explanation of what I hope to achieve.

I email it to her. Three days later she gives me a call. She informs me that the proposal is well written but she has a fundamental question. "Is this a memoir?" she asks.

I hadn't really thought about genre. But I guess my idea fits memoir. I didn't want to write an academic book arguing that racism still exists in workplaces; I wanted to tell my story. I guess that's what a memoir is—my story. "Yes," I said, far more confidently than I felt.

She continued her questions. "And what you want to talk about is . . ." She goes silent for a second. I assume she is checking her notes. ". . . white women touching your hair?"

"Yes," I say, this time actually feeling confident. "That's exactly what I want to talk about. I grew up in predominately white spaces and still struggled to succeed professionally. I suspect there are a lot of other Black women who are experiencing this, too, and I think I can give language to how it feels."

She is quiet for a moment before saying the words we all dread from someone dangling an opportunity in front of us: "I have to be honest . . ."

The air deflates from my lungs. I've been obsessively waiting for a response since I pushed SEND with my proposal and all my hopes attached. And now both are going to be rejected. I run my hand over the open notebook in front of me. The one with my details from that publishing meeting. The one with my notes as I developed the proposal. I close it. I know I won't need it to remember what she's going to say next.

"Austin, most memoirs are written by a celebrity. Or they are written by someone who has done something extraordinary. Someone who has climbed a mountain. Someone who has kicked a drug habit. Something . . . notable. I'm sorry, but I just don't think a book about white women touching your hair is going to sell."

"I understand," I say into the phone. "Thank you so much for taking a look at my proposal and chatting with me about it. It's been a true gift to see the inner workings of publishing."

I'm sure she can hear the disappointment in my voice. "Please don't give up," she says to me. "In fact, I would love to invite you for a tour of our publishing office." I think she is hoping I will write a new proposal, one that more closely aligns with the kinds of books they already have on shelves; one that makes an argument for the importance of racial justice. I don't really intend to write another proposal—ever—but I know this is a good opportunity, so I agree.

"I'd love to do that. Can I email you to set it up?" I respond.

When I hang up the phone, I have a profound sense of rejection, despite her encouragement. I am grateful for the opportunity to stay in communication with her, but I wish in my bones that it was to discuss my project.

I sit on the floor in front of my husband. He is in his office chair typing on his laptop. He stops, staring down at me.

"Tommie?" My voice is soft, tender. "I have to ask you a question."

"Okay," he responds, giving me his undivided attention. When I don't move from the floor, he knows I'm in emotional distress. "Come here, let's move to the bedroom."

I climb on the bed and pull my favorite purple blanket over my body, snuggling into the fuzzy softness.

"What's going on?" he asks.

I tell him about the conversation. My voice grows smaller and smaller under the heaviness I'm feeling.

"Tommie, do you think it's time for me to grow up? Is what I'm experiencing the Universe telling me that I need to let go of this dream of becoming a speaker or writer or doing diversity work at all? My dad has told me my entire life that I am capable of changing the world. And I really, really believed it. But is that all just a childish fantasy? Is it time for me to get a real job and put all of this away?" I motion toward my laptop and the notebook haphazardly tossed on top, my pen balancing on the edge.

In our relationship I am the butterfly, flitting from one project to another, always looking for an adventure. I am optimistic and believe that magic is always a possibility. I see clouds in the sky and wish away the rain. Tommie is steady and rooted. He looks at the sky, sees clouds, and expects the rain to fall. And he doesn't get particularly emotional about it.

I wait for him to give me a gentle but firm yes. I wait for him to tell me that he's always known there would be a moment when I had to stop chasing my ambitions and simply find a job that pays the bills. I wait for him to tell me that my adventurous days are over. I wait for him to tell me to be more like him—steady and rooted. I steel all my tender parts, and I wait for him to tell me to let go.

He finds my hand under the blanket. He looks in my eyes and says, "No. You have to keep going. You have to keep writing. It's who you are and who you are becoming."

Tears fall down my face. "You really believe that?" I ask, my voice all gravel, pleading with him to tell me the truth and not just what I am desperate to hear.

"Yes," he says. "Look at what your blog has already done. Look at how much it's grown. You wrote a book proposal. You met with an editor who sought you out. Of course, you have to keep going. Now, you might have to get another job or a few more jobs. You might have to submit multiple book proposals. You might have to write on this blog for a long time. But you absolutely have to keep going. It's not a figment of your imagination, babe. It's who you are."

My connection to a mentor opened a door, and my partner makes sure I don't close it. I am not swallowed by disappointment; I do not give up, because I am buoyed by them.

Torn

AS I CONTINUE to write, I do have to get another job. I am a college resident director, and I've just completed two weeks of training. Now it's the job of my team to train sixty or so resident assistants on campus rules and safety protocols. But I am distracted.

In the middle of these weeks of training, a town in Missouri has erupted. Initially, there aren't any news stories on what's happening down there. No journalists, no camera crews, just the people of Ferguson. For a day or two, community members sound the alarm that a police officer has killed an unarmed Black teenager and left him in the middle of the street for hours. They want justice, but no one is listening. So they start marching. And marching. And marching. They are using this new software called Periscope to livestream the protests, and for those paying attention, the videos become increasingly dystopic. By the time mainstream media show up, armored tanks are rolling past the McDonald's. Officers in combat gear brandish rifles and throw tear gas at Black folks outfitted in shorts and tank tops. Clergypeople leading peaceful protests are handcuffed and taken into custody.

I am doing an impossible balancing act. I am going

through the motions at work while my emotions are tied up with Ferguson. I lead my portion of a training but then return to my seat, searching for local updates about the case. I initiate volunteer opportunities in the community but check social media during the breaks to hear what activists are reporting. When my meetings are over, I stay in the room an extra ten minutes to watch any new videos that have emerged showcasing the marches.

It is a strange thing to try to bear witness to the Struggle all while keeping up the façade that my attention is solely focused only on the five feet in front of me. We—the Black community—are used to this balancing act. We have done it over and over again when a tragedy has rocked us and seemingly no one else. But for the first time, I can't do it. I can't pretend that I am singularly focused on work. I apologize for checking my phone. I apologize when I am late because I was writing or reading. I apologize for being sleepy because I stayed up late, again. Even after national news organizations catch up, I want the people of Ferguson to know they are not alone. I want to bear witness.

The people of Ferguson march for weeks. I am struck by how much energy bearing witness requires. Because it is not just watching. It is feeling. It is knowing. It is sharing a kinship with people I have never met and processing the disregard they are facing. It is shouting "Amen" and offering context to anyone willing to listen to the experiences of Black America. It is taking apart dog whistles like "The officer was afraid" and humanizing the victim when he is announced in *The New York Times* to be "no angel." Witnessing isn't passive. It is an act of meeting the moment, of being present to the pain, of knowing it could be any one of us next.

I am personally exhausted from moving to a new state, starting a new job, and trying to keep up with the recent wave of videos of unarmed Black men being shot by police. I'm not the only one. Many of us are tired. We have been trying to convince the country to pay attention. And now that they are, we still feel the need to be vigilant, to make sure racism doesn't get the last word on the reporting of Ferguson.

But life doesn't stop. I don't get to skip work meetings, so I find myself skipping meals. I don't get to skip trainings, so I find myself skipping social events. I don't get to travel down to Ferguson, so I find myself skipping sleep.

Of course, my struggle was nothing compared to that of the people who laced up tennis shoes and spent hours marching in the streets demanding justice. My struggle was nothing compared to being met with tear gas and military tanks. My struggle was nothing compared to the people who worked all day and marched all night. And so often, this is also what it means to be a Black woman in America: working during the day to put food on the table and then protesting all night to make America do better. It means splitting ourselves in half. This is what it's like to save ourselves.

One night I send a tweet, trying to make sense of how I

could be so tired without having set foot in Ferguson. I tweet about how I cannot fathom how tired the community must be. There is no way they are getting sleep as they work, meet, march, and do it again night after night. I tweet about how much this fight is taking out of all of us, and how very tired I am.

A Black woman tweets back. "You go to sleep, sis. I'll keep watch tonight."

It is a simple but profound moment for me, to feel held by someone I haven't met, but someone who knows exactly what I'm trying to say. Rather than engage me in an academic way—the way we often engage one another as we work out the cost of defying white supremacy in America— she responds to my need. And in that response, I understand what must be happening in Ferguson: this. One person sleeps and another person marches. One person watches the kids and another person cooks. One person hosts the meeting and another person eats. One person posts bail and another person holds the family. We don't just march together, fight together, write together, meet together. We also look out for one another and our physical needs. We remember that none of this is riding on one of us, and therefore we each can set it down and then come back. Prioritizing one another's survival in a system that doesn't honor our humanity is also how we practice solidarity.

I Love Myself When
I Am Looking Mean
and Impressive

How you like me now?

—ANCIENT BLACK
PROVERB, PROBABLY

Needs

THE WORLD HAD changed since I first submitted a book proposal. Ta-Nehisi Coates and Roxane Gay, both well-known writers, together proved that memoirs by noncelebrity Black folks could find a major readership. Ferguson forced the country to begin dealing with race in America as the protesters faced off with the state's national guard. And when three Black women coined the phrase Black Lives Matter, everyone began proclaiming the importance of listening to us. It was a time. And the publishing industry finally understood why it might be important to publish a book about a regular Black girl being tired of white women touching her hair. Well, they sort of understood.

I polish up my book proposal, and this time I submit it to more than one publishing house. Rather than being rejected, I receive offers from ten different publishers. My literary agent sets up meetings with all of them. She asks questions I don't entirely understand—questions about distribution, royalties, and rights—which she has to explain to me after the phone call. But that's as it should be, because I am doing my own translating during these meetings.

I thought submitting a book proposal would be the hard part. Turned out navigating the responses was like playing a decoding game. Despite the excitement conveyed in every meeting, I found myself having to determine if the editor wanted to publish the book I proposed or if they were more interested in adding my name to the graphic they'll create for Black History Month.

Of course, none of them said, "Austin, we think you're a decent writer, and we'd love to have your name on our 'books by diverse authors' list, but first you have to promise to tone it down." Instead, they said things like:

"It's our job to make sure you reach the widest possible audience and so when we go through the editing process we might make some suggestions you'll have to wrestle with."

"Perhaps it would be best if we avoided the use of the term 'white supremacy.' We want to make sure you don't scare away potential readers."

"What would you think of putting a glossary in the back of the book to explain some of the terms? For example, I'm not sure readers will know what the Middle Passage was. I didn't learn it until I was in graduate school."

On so many calls, white men and women had suggestions for how to write the right book on race, the one that would sell by making readers more comfortable, readers they invariably assumed would be white. It never occurred to them to wonder what book a Black woman—including its author—might need.

I sat in those meetings and smiled, refusing to make any verbal concessions. I did not negotiate. I did not compromise. I did not push back. I simply crossed their names off my mental list, with an absentminded "hmmmm," as if I was still paying attention.

I was new to the publishing world, but I had heard enough horror stories from women of color to know that this ruthless vetting was necessary. Each publishing house was telling me what book they *really* wanted me to write. Some wanted the book I proposed. Most wanted a book that painted racism in pretty pastels. But I would not soften my language to describe the impact of racism.

I did not care if some folks picked up my book, read a few paragraphs, and decided I was too mean for them to buy the book. Racism is mean, is malevolent. And I intended to match its energy. I chose a publishing house that had no problems when I wrote "White people can be exhausting" as my opening sentence. I wrote the book I needed.

Erased

I'M BACK IN a college classroom, this time for a conference. I take a seat and listen as the facilitator talks about a program he developed. In partnership with the college, his team offers men who are incarcerated an opportunity to earn a bachelor's degree. I'm highly interested in this program because I'm always looking for ways to undermine systems of injustice, until they can be abolished.

The college where I'm sitting is a bit of a unicorn. There are a handful of them sprinkled around the country: Christian at their core, conservative at their founding, but progressive compared to their counterparts, if you know where to look.

The classroom is filled to capacity: about forty people. We all sit quietly as we learn how this program was developed, how it got approved, and how it is sustained. It's a hopeful presentation focused on what those of us in the room can do to help upend the status quo and support the human dignity of those currently incarcerated.

As the facilitator closes, hands shoot up in the air. People are eager to engage. We are not new to this format. We know now is our chance to ask questions, and with a room this full, it's better not to be shy.

A woman with a long red ponytail goes first, asking more questions about the data. The facilitator answers that fifty degrees have already been handed out. She is followed by two men. One looks young enough to be a college student himself, and the other, middle aged, sports a button-down shirt tucked into belted jeans. Both want to know if the program is just a glorified Bible study—using academics as a façade for converting students to Christianity.

The answer is a clear no, and I can hear the relief of everyone in the room, as we quietly snicker at the irony of being Christians with no desires toward conversion. Every question is responded to as we all turn in our seats from question asker back to the front of the room, in anticipation of the answer. We are invested. Then a woman with a fluffy, purple scarf draped around her shoulders eagerly raises her hand.

When she is called on, she rises and offers her own lecture: "I know we are running out of time here, but I just have to express this. You've given a very good presentation about the program. But nowhere do you mention the racial statistics regarding incarceration and the criminal justice system. And that to me just seems egregious, especially when there are no Black people in the room. Everyone here needs to know that Black people are incarcerated at disproportionate rates . . ." She continues on, passionately laying out the racial disparities without noticing that half the room is no longer listening to her.

I can see her. She's just two rows over.

She does not see me.

The people in neighboring rows are staring at me. They are waiting to see how I'll respond. Will I interrupt her? Will I stand up and make my presence known? Will I raise my hand next and say something sarcastic or mean or kind or gracious? I'm used to having all eyes on me when I'm holding a microphone, but here, I just feel like a little kid who has been pointed out for being weird. I don't know where to look, so I keep my eyes trained on the facilitator.

We are not friends, the facilitator and I, but we have seen each other around the college, where we both work. He is unsure how to handle the moment. "Do you want me to address this?" he asks with the smallest turn of his neck, moving his face just an inch from center to his right. *Please don't, this is awkward enough*, I plead by swallowing hard and closing my eyes slowly, the movement too purposeful to be mistaken for blinking.

He turns back to the woman, who has now finished her diatribe. "Yes, I agree," he begins. "It is important to understand the racial history and the current racial realities of the incarceration system. And I would be happy to offer a list of resources for anyone interested in that topic. However, this particular lecture was focusing on our initiative. We felt pretty sure that anyone who chose this lecture over the others being offered concurrently is probably well versed in the racial inequities within the criminal justice system."

My mind is reeling. I'm bothered by being erased from

the room and simultaneously made the center of it. A moment ago I was deciphering in my head and heart how I might get involved. Now I am having a completely different conversation with myself. Trying to drop into my body to figure out what I want to do next, as opposed to what I think the white people around me are expecting I might do. "Double consciousness," as W.E.B. Du Bois called it, is a beast.

As the facilitator wraps up the discussion, everyone begins to gather their belongings. It's winter and there are many things to grab—brightly colored hats and coats, thick gloves and long scarves are all bunched up on our laps or oozing over the tops of tote bags. One white woman reaches across the desks and touches my hand. "I'm sorry," she says, simply but kindly, before exiting.

I'm desperately attempting to capture the thought I had before my presence became central in the room. I want to talk to the facilitator more about the program. How far away is it? What kind of volunteer opportunities are possible? Do you need a doctorate to participate?

I begin making my way to the front, trying not to trip over all the winter accoutrements or slip on the damp floor layered with melted snow. Before I can join the line to speak to the facilitator, the woman with all the statistics steps in front of me. She places one hand on my forearm and the other across her heart. She is gushing. "I'm so, so sorry," she begins. "I had no intention of erasing you as I was speaking. But I know my intentions are insignificant to the harm I may have caused. I do apologize. I just get so upset when no one is talking about how racist the system is and I just had to speak up. . . ."

I am overwhelmed by her. She has the language down. But she seems to have forgotten that I am a real human being and not a character in the story of her antiracism journey.

I think sometimes white people process our presence in their lives as depicted in movies—a Black best friend, a Black therapist, a Black mother figure—always at the ready to forgive, insert some wisdom, and point them in the right direction for their heroic mission. I feel the pull inside me, a habit that has often prioritized responding to the guilt of white people. But I don't have any special insight for this woman, and I don't want to pretend that I do. I'm trying to gain some insight for my own calling.

I feel determined. I know what I want. I want this conversation to end, so that I can have a conversation with the facilitator. She stresses a few more *sorry*s as she continues to explain, but I interject, "Would you excuse me? I want to catch our lecturer before he leaves." I extricate myself from her grasp and return to my own will.

"Can I ask you a few questions about the program?" I inquire as the woman's damp shoes squeak down the hallway.

Expert

IT'S THE SUMMER of 2016, and in just three weeks our campus will be buzzing with students again. As members of the residence life staff, we are meeting to begin our preparations, but this year is unlike the previous one. This year we have to discuss how we are going to moderate political discussions as they organically unfold outside the classroom—in the dormitories where we all live. Only three of us are present, so we catch up while waiting for the other seven to arrive.

Tara sits across from me. She is quiet but observant. Her eyes are always wide, taking in the people around her, but her observations are deeper than what she sees. She is consistently present to what is being felt within those near her. Her dark hair is pulled back in a ponytail, but her gray streak keeps falling in her face. Between us, at the head of the table is Ben. Ben is our supervisor. Older than Tara and I, he nonetheless has twice the energy of both of us combined. His energy is never frantic, and yet you suspect that if someone challenged him to a sprint at any moment, he would be ready. His general disposition is one of joy, and he is excited for a new school year.

November is roughly four months away, which means

everything is political. Even talking about the weather or what you plan to have for lunch is going to shape-shift into a conversation about the election. This conversation is no different.

We assess the political landscape together. Since we are all progressive, there is little danger that we'll dissolve into a debate, and so we engage freely, discussing how we feel. I lean forward and confess, "I'm pretty certain that Trump is going to be president."

Tara's face flinches, but otherwise she doesn't move a muscle. She is taking me in. But Ben laughs hard. His entire face turns red as he falls back against his chair. "Noooo," he objects between chuckles.

Ben's laughter is entirely reasonable, or at least we all hope it's reasonable. Most political pundits agree with him, and the polling has Trump behind opponent Hillary Clinton. I once laughed, too, at the suggestion, until Trump decided not to denounce the endorsement of David Duke and remained in the running for President of the United States. In that moment, I suspected this could be the phenomenon Dr. Michelle Alexander alludes to in her book *The New Jim Crow:* the backlash whiteness would hand down for electing a Black president twice. Unfortunately, those concerns intensify every time I drive between major cities—from Grand Rapids to Detroit, from Ann Arbor to Toledo, from Chicago back to Grand Rapids. The small Midwest towns along the way are filled with eight-foot banners shouting their support for a candidate endorsed by a grand wizard of the Ku Klux Klan.

Not to mention, white people are pretty good at hiding their real selves from one another. But as a Black woman on the internet, I know what Ben doesn't. Some of the same white people laughing along with him at dinner tables and church picnics are in my direct messages, telling me exactly what they think about the "racial progress of the country."

I exist in a body onto which white people project their political fears, fears which they are often eager to share with much vulgarity.

Ben's laughter isn't derisive or mean. He just wants to believe that the idea was ludicrous. Because he doesn't know white people like I know white people. And this is the difficulty of being a Black woman.

Ben wasn't dismissing me that day, but in other rooms my understanding of how the world functions has been derided. I have been deemed cynical. I have been deemed bitter. I have been deemed hopeless. I have been told I need a change in attitude; I need to work on being more optimistic, like my white coworkers (the word "white" always remains unspoken, of course). My opinion is considered unreliable because it is based on an understanding that white people do not possess of themselves. Black people, especially Black women, are told we have an attitude problem when what we actually have is insider information.

Tara's reaction is different from Ben's. She looks from

Ben to me. She notices that I am not laughing. All she finds on my face is a raised eyebrow, slightly surprised that Ben is laughing so hard. "Do you really think so?" she asks earnestly, giving me an opportunity to share more.

Tara trusts me. We have worked closely together for a couple years. We have been through Ferguson and Walter Scott, through Mother Emanuel and Freddie Gray. We watched Eric Garner's murderer go free and Laquan McDonald shot sixteen times. We watched confederate flags come down and a vitriolic response fire up. Tara knows that I'm no prophet. I don't have a crystal ball in my back pocket. I'm just a Black woman sharing what I can't unsee. And perhaps for the first time, I am believed.

I was right, but that's not what's important here. Because I have also been wrong. Very wrong.

In July 2024 we are gearing up for another election. Donald Trump is once again the head of the Republican party despite his continued incompetence. On the Democrats' side is an aging Joe Biden—and many voters seem to want someone younger. There is talk about putting Vice President Kamala Harris at the top of the ticket.

When someone asks my opinion on the matter, I write in no uncertain terms, "A Black woman is not going to be President of the United States unless her name is Michelle Obama . . . or maybe Oprah."

At that moment in time I had no expectation that the Democratic party was capable of the kind of unity that would be required to make a Black woman the presidential nominee, and I wasn't sure I wanted them to be. I assumed that if we changed the ticket, there would be a free-for-all. Anyone with presidential aspirations would run, assuming themselves to be a better option than a Black woman. There would be confusion, and the particular combination that is racism and sexism doesn't require much confusion to stop progress in its tracks.

I was also concerned about the cost. Over eight years, we watched the two terms of the Obamas give rise to birtherism, comics of Michelle Obama as a monkey, and a continuous onslaught of disrespect rooted in racism. How would they treat a Black female president? What would this job require of her? What would it require of Black women to weather through her term?

For me, the prospect spelled danger. Danger for her. Danger for a lot of Black women who would now be subject to the crass political tactics that would surely be used to try to take her down.

Just weeks later, the opposite of all that I expected had happened. President Joe Biden stepped down. Kamala Harris stepped up, and the Democratic party with her. It was extraordinary to witness in real time as congressional members and former presidents threw their unwavering support behind her in the weeks that followed. But it doesn't change the fact that I got that one very, very wrong. She did face a number of racist attacks and didn't win the election, but she came closer than I thought was possible in my lifetime.

Whether or not the predictions of Black women turn out

to be correct isn't the point. What's more important is that our concerns and convictions are believed to have merit, to be worth consideration. I have no desire to be anyone's magical negro, incapable of my intuition being wrong. My declaration of what's possible in 2016 or 2024 is not meant to be a cosmic warning or an exercise of inborn brilliance. I meant only to convey my concern.

In conference rooms all over this country, Black women are voicing concerns about policies and goals. We are voicing concerns about vision and mission. We are voicing concerns about budgets and mandates. We are voicing concerns about decisions that could prove to be harmful. We do not do this as an exercise of cynicism but as an act of hope that a better choice could be made.

I dream of a world where Black women are regarded as well-reasoned. Where the point we are trying to make or the concern we want to convey is given the consideration we deserve. I wonder what it would look like for those around us to be affected by our analysis. Until this world exists, I suppose we will simply have to be impressed with ourselves.

PowerPoint

IT'S THE SUMMER of 2020, and corporate America is eager to prove they are making strides in their commitments to diversity and inclusion. I am entering my third virtual conference for the day, and this time a team of consultants is staring back at me through my screen. They represent a manufacturing company in the Midwest that has hired me to talk about diversifying their leadership team. This is a premeeting with the consultants to learn more about the client before I lead my workshop with them.

I dive in with my own questions to ascertain how I can be of help. "Can you tell me more about the racial makeup of the company?" I ask.

One of the three faces smiling back at me answers the question. "Well, it's actually pretty diverse. This company has a workforce that's 80 percent Hispanic."

I am stunned. "Eighty percent?" I repeat, not bothering to hide my shock. When a company struggles to increase their leadership diversity, it's usually because there is a lack of diversity in the overall organization. But this company has an abundance.

"Yes," they confirm. So, I ask another question.

"Can you tell me about the racial makeup of the executive committee or leadership team as it stands now?"

"Well," they say, "the executive committee is all white."

I try not to make assumptions. The executive committee could be three people. I am wondering if I can solve this by just telling them to double the size of the committee and add three people from the 80 percent Brown workforce. There is no way there aren't three qualified people who have the tenure and expertise to lead; the company won't even have to make outside hires if they don't want to.

"How big is the executive committee?" I ask.

"There are currently fourteen people on the committee."

"Huh!" is the only response I can manage. *Well, damn. Guess my solution isn't going to work after all.* I'm intrigued to learn more about what is happening systemically at this company to cause such a phenomenon. They certainly cannot claim to be unable to find people of color. I want to meet these folks. I believe they could fix this problem tomorrow and inspire their workforce with deepened trust, buy-in, and communication once they do. I'm brimming with curiosity and hope.

Now the consultants have a few questions for me. They ask about my book and a little about my pedagogy. I try to be honest with people about what to expect from me as a racial justice educator. It has taken me years to embrace my own style of presenting. I enjoy bringing clarity to vague ideas, and I would much rather do a Q & A than deliver a lecture. I rarely read from a script, and I have a hard time not walking (and waving and jumping and bending and flipping my hair) while I talk.

I explain that I am a storyteller. I am good at giving examples, making systemic racism visible. I'm good at answering questions where knowledge and practice meet. I am really good at giving space for people of color to speak for themselves, which is often the most valuable information an organization can receive while discussing inclusion. I'm good at refocusing, re-envisioning, and reinvigorating the pursuit toward racial justice.

When I'm finished, one of the consultants responds, "That sounds great. Can we see your presentation slides in advance? And could you forward us any additional handouts you plan to use?"

"Oh, I don't have any," I respond. "But each participant should bring a notebook and come with at least two questions they have regarding antiracism efforts within their company."

There is a heavy silence. All three faces stare back at me.

"I'm sorry, did you say there won't be a presentation?"

"I will definitely be presenting, but, no, there won't be a deck or a PowerPoint," I explain. "I'm going to introduce myself and talk about the work of antiracism for twenty minutes or so. And then I'm going to open the floor so we can talk more specifically about the barriers this team faces toward setting or enacting its own goals."

The faces continue to watch me.

"Ummm . . . our clients will expect there to be a Power-Point presentation."

I can see them growing uncomfortable. Another voice jumps in. "Austin, do you think you could create just two or three slides? It doesn't have to be anything elaborate, but it would really help our client."

I lean back in my chair, considering whether this is something I am willing to do. I don't want to be made to feel like less of an "expert" because I don't present using slides, case studies, journal articles, or other scholarly trappings. But I also want to be of service to any client in front of me. I'm genuinely searching myself, silently weighing if there is a way to agree to their request without betraying who I am.

Before I can offer a response, someone else jumps in. "Our client will expect there to be some sort of presentation or handout. This is how they assess if you are in fact an expert in your field."

All three are starting to shift in their seats. There is an increasing urgency in their voices; I can see their eyes moving around the screen, looking at one another. They are panicking.

I try once more to express the importance of how I lead during these kinds of gatherings. I even offer to create one or two slides, but I warn them, "There is every possibility that I won't follow my own outline. My brain is always going to prioritize the conversation unfolding in front of me. I'm not really interested in proving my expertise as much as I am interested in responding to the particularities of the group that hired me." I'm trying to be forthright and head off any problems that may occur on the back end if I don't stick to my admittedly superficial slides.

Their faces scrunch up with concern before they repeat how utterly important it is that I prove myself this way. I can sense their rising urgency, but their overuse of the word "expert" has caught my attention. I have my antiracism hat on, and I'm too busy assessing what I'm witnessing to calm them down.

"You know," I answer, "I am very intrigued that your client's workforce is predominately Brown but that such a large executive team is entirely white. Through this conversation I think I'm beginning to understand why. If the committee truly believes there is only one way to show an expert level of understanding, this may be a primary barrier that has prevented them from being able to see what 80 percent of their workforce could bring to the table in a leadership role."

The white woman explodes, as if I'd offended her. "I don't think it's at all unreasonable to expect an educator to come to the table with a presentation and handouts." She places emphasis on all the nouns in her sentence.

"I'm not suggesting it's unreasonable," I state. "I am suggesting that the deep belief that there is only one right way to prove one's authority and value may be evidence of why this company is struggling with diversifying its leadership team."

The woman is aghast. The two men on the call know they can't save this impasse. It doesn't matter; I'm ready to end the conversation.

What started for me as interest about how fast this organization could turn things around morphs into dread. I could be committing myself to a waste of time and energy. Based on the way the consultants feel the need to protect them, I'm not at all convinced the company is actually ready to make changes.

I cancel the contract. At the end of the call, I notify them to find another antiracism educator. I imagine they would have done the same anyway. I imagine they found me to be quite mean. And I love that for myself.

Once upon a time, I would have created a fifteen-slide presentation while they were still on the call to prove my own expertise. Once upon a time, their opinion of what made a "true" educator would have lodged itself right in the center of my chest. Once upon a time, I would not have considered my own boundaries or valued my experience enough to fight for it. I would not have defended my uniqueness.

Now let me pause here to add that my reaction was also rooted in a very particular luxury called "financial freedom," born of becoming a freelance writer and speaker. I did not count on this client for a recurring check. These folks could not hold my benefits hostage. I would never have to sit before them for a performance review. I would not be expected to have lunch with them later that day.

There was no group project in our future. Because of this, they lost their power to make their reality my reality. I was able to hold on to what makes me impressive. I was able to risk being considered mean.

In every workplace I have occupied, white people have gotten away with being rude because they were in a hurry, or mean because they were going through a lot, or aggressive because their anger was evidence that they cared deeply. On the other hand, Black women must walk on eggshells. To one degree or another, we are expected to reach the bar of "pleasant," and it's preferrable that we always be reaching for "likable."

But I am pretty sure likability is impossible. In essential terms, we must empty ourselves in order to be likable.

In my work career I tried a lot of things to be likable. I tried to read off beat, but my body wouldn't let me. I tried to be a bridge, but I couldn't let people walk all over me. I subconsciously altered the octave of my voice, but because I wouldn't change what I had to say, I was always making them uncomfortable. I tried to participate in conversations, but my honest opinion was never valued and I couldn't endorse theirs. I tried to smile and nod my way through retreats in the middle of nowhere, and still my facial expressions directed to the other Black girl gave me away. I couldn't sacrifice myself. And so I had to be mean, which really just meant being myself. Since I can't be likable, I might as well be free.

Moving On

I'M SITTING IN a sterile room, growing my baby boy in my belly. I am overwhelmed by the realization that I am going to become a mother, a title I was never sure I'd hold. What I don't know is that I am also suffering from perinatal depression. I know that I am quieter, more emotional, always on the verge of tears. I watch ridiculous TV filled with unnecessary drama—the only shows I can watch that make me feel something. My back hurts. I struggle to climb into bed and struggle to climb out of it when I have to pee, which is all the time. I am finally over throwing up every day, but I'm still surprised by the smells that make me nauseous: everything from alfredo sauce to my husband's cologne can send me running to the nearest trash can.

At this point I have lost count of the doctors' appointments. My husband is with me, and I am always grateful when he is. I dread going to these things alone because my anxiety launches into overdrive. I forget my questions or I become tongue-tied, debating whether I really want to know the answers. Maybe ignorance is bliss. Every checkup feels like a test. Am I eating enough? Am I eating right? Am I moving my body enough? How is my iron? Is the baby's heartbeat okay? I'm hoping for an A, but I am overwhelmed by the number of things I am expected to control. Why does it constantly feel like this is something I could mess up?

Only a few of the medical folks are rude or brash. Most are lighthearted and acknowledge the fear seeping through my pores, if only by pausing after I respond "I'm fine," giving me an opportunity to say more, if I want to.

The most memorable appointment comes with a white woman whose long brown hair is tied up in a butterfly clip. She chats about living in Grand Rapids and manages to name a couple people we have in common, all vocal proponents of racial justice. Grand Rapids has that small community feel. She is chatty and asks us where we live and if we enjoy our jobs and if we plan to stay in the area after our son is born.

We tell her we live just south of Grand Rapids, but that we will be moving to Detroit soon. We tentatively explain that we prefer not to raise our boy in this mostly conservative, definitely culturally white town.

"Oh no." She turns away from her computer screen to look at us both. "You can't move. We need you. These white people need you here, need your family here. It's the only way it's going to change."

My husband and I glance at one another. This happens to us a lot where we live: white people making pronouncements about race. It happened when a white electrician walked into our apartment and felt the need to inform us that he knows some Black people live in nice homes and some white people are poor and don't have nice homes. It happened when we were killing time in the convenience store looking at magazine covers, and a white man asked us about Jesse Jackson before launching into his assessment of whether hip-hop is good for the Black community.

But now we are in a doctor's office, and the last thing we are looking for is a pronouncement on our duty to white people. My husband looks directly at me. I can read his face: *Do you want me to tell this white woman that this conversation is exactly why we're moving?*

I turn back to her, a little smile playing at the corners of my lips because I know my husband well. I ask, "Can we talk more about the baby?"

I am less annoyed because I am not alone, but the truth is I am sick of white people telling me that I have to remain in unhealthy workplaces, unhealthy worship spaces, unhealthy towns, in order to save them. Everywhere I go, I am told that I should sacrifice myself for the possibility of whiteness getting its shit together.

And I have done exactly that over and over again. I have stayed at jobs that tore me apart. I have stayed in classrooms that ignored me. I have stayed in conference rooms that dismissed me. I have stayed in meetings that silenced me. I have stayed. Not because I thought I deserved the mistreatment but because I was told this is what the sacrifice for racial justice looks like: convincing white people to be better humans.

I'm done with that now. They are going to have to make that choice on their own.

After the baby was born, we moved to one of America's chocolate cities, Detroit. We do not exist to save white people from themselves.

The Rider

THUS FAR, WRITING on my blog has garnered me a couple small gigs and a handful of writing opportunities in online religious magazines. But then I get a call. A popular women's conference wants me to be a speaker. This conference usually has an all-white-woman lineup, but as those women become more exposed to voices beyond their inner circles (thank you, social media!) Black women find ourselves accepting more and more opportunities.

Even while I lament the lack of diversity at these conferences, I admire many of the women who speak at them. They are finding their own way, creating careers they love, leading growing businesses while rewriting the traditional rules of caring for a family. It's inspiring. I have attended conferences like this one and enjoyed myself, but I always wished I didn't have to translate their experiences into mine. Now I'll be able to speak to the women of color like me, who attend these conferences but want to see themselves represented, too.

This will be one of my first big conferences, one that tours to multiple cities. Eventually it was time to submit my rider . . . after I wrote one. A rider is intended to inform the hosts about the speaker's needs. Celebrity riders can be specific to the point of requesting 3 liters of Coke Zero, 27 straws, a temperature of 72.5 degrees, and a blue-and-orange-striped chair. But most of us who are not being vied for keep it pretty simple: a flight, a hotel stay, and if you're feeling fancy, a car service. Mine was simple.

When I make my submission, I am told they aren't accepting anyone's rider. Since this is a multicity tour, with various speakers and artists at each stop, managing everyone's rider will be too much. Instead, they plan to offer the same standard services to everyone: flight, hotel, and a group greenroom with snacks available for all speakers.

I happily signed the contract and waited for the first tour stop. I rocked that stage. It was a good time. And it made me happy to be a part of diversifying the conference, of being able to literally say to other Black women in the audience, "I see you."

When the evening is over, I share an Uber back to the hotel where all the speakers are staying. I've known my cab mate for a long time but haven't seen her in a couple years. I am excited to catch up with her. We are talking about our experience of the conference when she flips her bleach blonde hair over her shoulder and says, "Oh, and it is always so nice when hosts actually read the rider and deliver, right?" My face scrunches up in response. She interprets my confusion as wanting to know what was in her rider, so she continues, "You know, like having a car service. I mean, doesn't it just make things easier when you know exactly who is coming to get you and what time—especially at the hours we have to be at the airport."

I close my eyes and sigh.

Of course. Of course, they accepted riders from some speakers but not others. Not speakers like me. All the talk about equality and togetherness was hiding the continuation of status and power. Who was important enough to submit their riders, their requests, their expectations, and who should just be glad to be invited? It sucks when white women want to celebrate our shared womanhood and still deny my personhood, by lying to me and upholding the same rigid hierarchies used against all of us. I believed we were all being treated equally; I thought that was part of what we were all celebrating. I thought we were turning the system upside down. Turns out the system was still sitting on me and the other marginalized women who had been invited.

I decided right then, as I watched the city pass by, that I would never let white feminism use me again. I would not accept invitations where I was the only woman of color. "Verify" became my favorite word as I defied privacy expectations. I reached out to other speakers to *verify* what I was told about contracts, *verify* riders, *verify* payments and other details of events. And then I kept expanding my verification process. I spoke with conference planners before accepting an event to be sure my content would not be censored. I verified that I would not be the only person representing all marginalized voices. I verified that I would be safe and there would be a plan for security. I risked being impolite, risked being forthright. I'd rather be rude than used.

I Love Myself When I Am Awkward

what did i see to be
except myself?

—LUCILLE CLIFTON,
"WON'T YOU
CELEBRATE WITH ME"

Pleather

AS A KID, I am obsessed with books. I always have a just-in-case book with me . . . just in case we get stuck in traffic, just in case the line at the grocery store is long, just in case my parents run into someone they know. Like many kids, I adore Judy Blume and Shel Silverstein. I love the wordplay of Amelia Bedelia and bounce back and forth between YA and adult fiction. My mother has only two rules when it comes to choosing books: (1) If I can understand it, I can read it. (2) If I have questions, come talk to her. That's it. I often reach for Pearl Cleage, Toni Morrison, and other authors the Black women in my life are reading.

I'm a nerd who loves the fantasy world of books, and sometimes I forget I don't live in one. I'm generally able to hide some of this whimsicality, because I attend schools that require uniforms. Most days everyone looks the same. But every now and then, we receive a free day—the opportunity to wear anything we want. And in those moments, "hidden" is the last way anyone would describe me.

By eleven or twelve I am already the same height as my mother, which means I can raid her closet on free days. In it I find all kinds of treasures, including black-and-white-striped bell-bottoms made of spandex and jersey. I am entranced by the flair at the bottom. When I spin in circles, they flair out even more, turning me into a human optical illusion. They are loud and quirky, and I love them. I pair them with a silver chain-link belt. The alternating triangles and circles drape beautifully over my soon-to-emerge hips. The belt makes a charming clink every time I move.

I have a photo of my mother as a teenager. She is sitting at my grandmother's dining room table, peering up at the camera through black cat-eye glasses. I wish I had those glasses, instead of the clear plastic ones swallowing my face right now. They are screaming nineties as streaks of purple, gold glitter, and flecks of teal fill the plastic frames with no discernible pattern or intention. Nonetheless, I am glad to be out of uniform and wearing something that makes me feel amazing.

. . . until I arrive at school and see the looks on everyone's faces. My friends. My teachers. The administrators. Everyone I come into contact with that day seems perplexed. Even the Lunch Ladies struggle to come up with a way to comment on my bell-bottoms—something that isn't a compliment but also doesn't leave a bemused silence sitting between us. No one says they are cool. No one asks me where I got them from. Everyone just blinks at me with eyebrows raised, like they, too, have become entranced by the optical illusion but do not enjoy it. All day I fixate on my pants. I am determined to delight in them, because I know I am never, ever going to wear them again.

I did it again in high school. I was so excited when the school announced our first uniform-free day. I just knew everyone was as excited as I was to get out of our ill-fitting clothes into something that truly spoke to us. I imagined our entire school would transform into a fashion show. We would strut up and down the hallways turning them into runways. We would pose for an imaginary camera before twirling into our classrooms. We would high-five one another and snap our fingers in approval of everyone's choices.

I was wrong.

Every student, all sixteen hundred of them, shows up in jeans and a T-shirt. Except me. I'm wearing beige pleather pants, stiff and shiny, looking more like plastic than leather. On top, I am sporting a matching pleather jacket that barely bends at the elbows. It's belted with a double row of silver grommets. The same large grommets decorate the pockets and notched collar. As I walk through the halls, it feels like a spotlight is following me. In my mind, I have just become the nerdy girl in the movies who everyone is laughing at as she passes by.

At first I try to carry myself with confidence: head up, shoulders back, eyes straight ahead. I add a little switch to my walk, feigning self-assurance. But as the day wears on, my posture falters. My friends tease me gently with an "Oh, okay, ma'am" or "Oh, so that's how we do, huh?" I laugh good-naturedly, but I am mortified. I can't believe it never occurred to me to just wear jeans and a T-shirt. How am I the only person out of sixteen hundred who didn't get the memo?

By lunchtime I cannot keep up this façade any longer. Before heading to the cafeteria, I stop at my locker, yanking at my sleeves. I remove the jacket and stuff it inside, trying not to cry because I can't do anything about my pants.

Most people know that I'm a good student. They know I'm a wallflower at dances. They know there is not one rap song I could recite from beginning to end—including the ones I like. They know I am active at church and lead a Bible study once a week. They know I'm my own brand of quirky, and I've made peace with that. But standing out physically is too much for me. All my bravery is already spread thin. Every now and then, I just want to blend in, but apparently blending is not my strong suit.

A Series of Awkward Events

MY INTROVERTED NATURE is completely at odds with my love for being onstage. Hand me a microphone and I am effortlessly confident and calm. I feel powerful there, completely self-possessed. I cannot help but wonder if the stage is my happy place, because in regular life I am awkward as hell. For years I have tried to convince myself that my awkwardness is the natural but temporary result of growing pains. From the night of prom, I began reckoning with the possibility that awkward might just be my middle name.

My date is Myles Johnson, an elementary school friend who I've known forever. If our classroom was a sitcom, he would have been the class clown—but better, because he never tried to be funny. He just was. Once, in the middle of science class, Busta Rhymes's "Put Your Hands Where My Eyes Could See" was stuck in his head. He started singing it. When he got to his favorite part, he added jerky arm movements like he was performing in the music video. It was so random, I couldn't help but laugh. When he gave one good bounce too many, his brown folding chair collapsed right under him. I could hardly breathe from laughing so hard. He was great, and I couldn't wait to hang with him at the dance.

For the first time, I resist the temptation to hold up the walls. I join Myles on the dance floor as we bust out every old-school dance we can think of. It's a good time. After the dance is when things fall apart, and quickly.

We are all required to attend the school's after-party, an attempt to keep us from making questionable decisions after prom. This year the after-party is held at a huge recreation center. And that is where my awkwardness decides to take center stage.

As I prepared for prom, I considered every detail of my dress and bra and hair and jewelry and shoes—everything. But I gave not one thought to the transition to after prom. And it showed. Because I was glued to the passenger seat in the car doing a lot of overthinking.

The trouble began when it occurred to me I had no idea where I was supposed to change from my prom dress into my jeans and T-shirt. I knew they wouldn't let me leave once we got inside. So what would I do with my dress (and all the garments under my dress) once I finished changing? I decided the best course of action was just to change in the car. It was dark, and I knew Myles would stand guard.

I wiggle out of my stockings and slip my jeans on easily. But when I try to pull my dress over my head, I get stuck. (Oh yeah, I safety-pinned my strapless bra to my dress.) I try for a couple minutes to undo the pins, but to no avail. The safety pins are tiny. They must be the safest safety pins on the planet. I can't see them in the dark, and even when I catch them in the moonlight, my new acrylic nails at this moment feel like the claws of an animal. I'm sweating. I'm not particularly well endowed, so I make the decision to go without a bra. I begin to pull my dress and the attached bra over my head again . . . and get stuck a second time. I forgot I still have to unsnap my bra, even if I can't unpin it from my dress.

For a moment I consider asking Myles for help, but I can't figure out how to ask him to unsnap my bra in a way that sounds platonic. With the fabric of my dress bunched around my shoulders, I lean back, keeping it out of the way while I wiggle one hand underneath, pulling the bra low enough to reach the hooks. I'm trying hard not to draw Myles's attention by grunting out loud, but I am certain that grunting would help immensely. Finally, I get it undone. Off goes the dress, on goes my T-shirt, and I'm ready.

We enter the recreation center, which has been converted into a playful indoor carnival. We dance for a bit in front of the DJ and then walk to the next station. That's when I notice the giant pile of gym bags all the girls brought with them for changing out of their dresses. Gym bags. What a novel idea for concealing undergarments.

We head over to make giant bubbles and play a couple of games. We take pictures every few minutes as the people around us click disposable cameras. I'm having a blast, but I need to use the restroom. When I emerge from the stall, I take in my reflection in the mirror. My makeup is still flawless and my hair hasn't budged despite the gymnastics in the car. But my eyes travel over my clothes, and that's when I realize I've had my shirt on backwards for two hours. I knew it felt a little tight around my neck . . .

I'm staring in the mirror thinking about all the pictures I have taken. In all of them everyone is wearing the same T-shirt, and mine is backwards. Evidence. There is permanent evidence of my mistake. I shake my head and silently yell at myself. *Austin, Austin, Austin, girl. Why are you like this?*

I reenter the stall and fix my shirt. I give myself one more scan in the mirror, making sure my pants are zipped and there isn't toilet paper glued to my body somewhere. Despite my embarrassment, everything looks fine.

As we continue wandering around the recreation center, I am hopeful that I have endured all the awkward moments I can handle, and the rest of the night will be smooth sailing. Those hopes are dashed when I lose my weave in the middle of an inflatable obstacle course. The moment I'm clutching my weave in my fist is the moment I know for sure I am an awkward Black girl.

For years I have tried to erase this awkward, quirky version of myself. I have yelled at her to get it together. I have waited impatiently to shed her like a snake sheds its skin, hoping for the moment when I could step over her and leave her behind. I have waited to outgrow her, biding my time for sophistication to crowd her out. I have been frustrated at her existence time and time again. I have tried to empty myself of her, when what I needed most was to embrace her.

I wish I could share a single story in which I finally made peace with this part of myself. The truth is I am still working on it. I am still embracing my own contradictions—that I am a girl who can stand onstage and inspire an audience to tears, but I also might lose my weave in the parking lot.

Just last spring, I was getting ready to walk onstage when one of my eyelashes started peeling off. At that moment, an attendee spotted me and asked for a picture. I didn't want to disappoint, so I asked her if she could give me two seconds to rip my eyelashes off and put them in my purse. She was happy to oblige, and without a single judgmental remark.

I contain multitudes. Even though it's hard, I am learning to embrace the part of me that refuses to get its shit together, the part of me that is always out of line, always a little crooked. I am learning to make space for her, because she is a part of my humanity, too. May we live in a world where all Black women can make space for the multitudes we contain and be surrounded by people who have chosen to love all of us—not just when we are impressive, but when we are awkward and falling apart, too.

The Salon

NOTHING SPIKES MY anxiety like walking into a new hair salon. From the moment I hear that little bell announce my arrival, something Pavlovian happens as my brain and body become enemies. When the whole place goes silent because everyone naturally turned to the door, my brain screams *You in danger, girl,* in Whoopi Goldberg's voice. This is the moment I typically trip over the black mat on the floor. I see the mat. But my brain is screaming *Run* while I try to walk with some measure of confidence, and my body gets confused.

I do everything wrong in the salon. I stay under the hooded dryer that is no longer drying, trying to telepathically connect with my stylist. I am notorious for not following the stylist to her station when I am supposed to. I can't remember my left from my right as she tells me where to sit, so I plop in the wrong chair, of course.

Even after I'm seated in the stylist's chair, my anxiety won't calm down. I am rendered unable to tell her exactly what I want. I am overcome by shyness. I struggle to make simple decisions—do I want a trim? Curls or straight? Part on the left or right? By the third question, I feel like a walking inconvenience, and contemplate finishing my hair at home.

I usually make it out of these situations relatively unscathed, but every now and then, this tendency toward shyness kicks my butt, like the first time I get crochet twists installed.

I'm already nervous about the type of twists I've purchased. Some were prelooped and some were not. The thickness varied considerably. There were several lengths and types, and I didn't know what any of these differences meant for the style itself. So I took a guess.

I arrive at the shop and manage to avoid tripping over the mat. I sit in the wrong seat for only a few seconds. When I inform my braider I want crochet twists, she responds, "Okay. So how would you like me to cornrow your hair?"

My mouth falls open, but nothing intelligent comes out. My face is blank. She gives me a couple options, but my brain screams, *You don't know what you're doing!*

I'm not sure if she eventually decides or if I pick one. But a decision has been made and I pull out the twists. She opens one pack and immediately says, "These are the wrong ones." *Dammit.*

"Next time get the ones that say 'prelooped,'" she instructs. I nod dutifully and sink farther down into my chair. This is a disaster. I might as well get up and purposefully trip over the mat at this point.

She cornrows my hair into a circle pattern. She tucks the

twists into each row. When she is finished, she turns my seat around so I can look in the mirror. Staring back at me is a live version of an eighties Cabbage Patch doll. It looks like yarn is growing out from my head in thick knots. And because my hair is cornrowed into a circle, there is no place to put a part. So my twists keep flopping forward in my face.

"Um. Do you like this?" my braider asks skeptically.

My smile is tight as I attempt to lie. "Hmm," I say.

"You do like it?" she asks again to my nonresponse.

My anxiety was already at peak levels from this whole experience. I am a ball of nerves. *Just get out of here,* my brain screams. *Get out. Get out. Get out.*

"I think it's okay," I say politely.

She is in disbelief. She knows I hate it. She hates it. If anyone else had been in the shop that day, they would have instructed her to *take that mess out of my hair.* But there were no bold women in the shop that day. Just me.

I pay and leave. I drive straight to my favorite bookstore and try to calm down. I can't actually focus enough to read any of the book titles, but I feel safer as I meander through the bookish world I know. On a nearby rack is a row of reading glasses and a tiny mirror. I bend over to look in the mirror and almost laugh. I look so ridiculous, I can't even take myself seriously. I've never left a bookstore so fast.

Once at home, I text my braider. "I tried. But I can't do it. How soon can you get me in for a new style?" The next day I am in her chair with the right twists.

I wish I could have been able to say "This don't look

right" from the jump. In fact, I wish I could have simply asked: "How will the cornrow pattern impact the style?" But sometimes social anxiety just screams too loud. I can't hear anything else over it.

And so I have learned to prepare for my social anxiety by inviting a trusted friend into it. The next time I have an appointment at a new salon, I bring Zakiya with me. I tell her about my social anxiety and how it sometimes takes my brain a long time to answer even simple questions honestly. Zakiya is far more extroverted than I am, and she is willing to use her extroversion to give my rational voice time to speak up.

When the stylist asks me a question, I look at Zakiya. Z repeats the question. Or she'll make a joke. Or she'll explain why the decision matters. She gives my brain time to ascertain there is no need to panic. If I am unsure and need to talk out my answer, she is the sounding board. She gently asks "Are you sure?" giving me a chance to change my mind if I did feel pressured to make a decision before I was truly ready.

Turns out the best thing I can do to love my quirkiness is not to deny its existence but to invite my people into it.

Goofy

MOST SATURDAY AND Sunday mornings, Dr. Melissa Harris-Perry graces our TV screen. Her politics show is the kind my partner and I have been waiting for. For years we have listened to the white male talking heads explain what's happening in Washington. We listen to their observations and spend the rest of the week correcting their narratives or adding more meat where the tendon of an idea has some merit.

But Dr. Harris-Perry's show is different. She feels no need to divorce her lived experiences as a Black woman from her expert opinions. She invites guests that we never see on other shows—her fellow Black women academics, journalists, and artists. She is equally concerned about what's happening in the government and about what's happening in pop culture. In fact, she excels at drawing connections between the two. We love it.

One morning as I'm watching MHP, she shares a personal story. As I remember it, she tells her audience that she was recently in a meeting with her TV production colleagues and supervisors. Everyone must take a few minutes to introduce themselves and share something that makes them stand out—the usual icebreaker. When it's her turn, MHP chooses to describe her unique feature as "goofy."

She pauses before sharing their reaction. The folks around the table spend the next few minutes correcting her. "Goofy?" one responds. "No, no, you are serious." "Yes, and intellectual," another offers. They share all the words they want to trade out for her. She looks straight into the camera and says, "My colleagues aren't entirely wrong. I am serious and intellectual and a number of other words they offered. But I am also goofy," she says emphatically.

She then offers on-air evidence of her propensity to be goofy. Cycling through clips of past episodes, she chronicles antics like wearing tampon earrings. But I am lost in my head, or maybe my heart.

My whole life I've been on the lookout for people trying to tell me who I am. But I have never considered how often people have tried to tell me, and other Black women, who we are not. In that moment, something clicks in my chest.

Whiteness really likes serious Austin. It likes me when I am a good student. It likes me when I am a quiet employee. It likes me when I help others shine. It likes me when it can define me in ways that serve it. But it doesn't like me when I am goofy.

It doesn't like me when I am silly, when I am hysterical. It doesn't like me when I am feral, when I am a loose cannon. It doesn't like me when I laugh too loudly or for too long. It doesn't like me when I am playful or giddy. It doesn't like me when I am free. "This is not who you are," it urges with feigned concern. But like MHP, I'm learning to delight in all of me . . . especially my antics.

I Love Myself When I Am Embodied

I am a beautiful woman

—NIKKI GIOVANNI,
"EGO-TRIPPING"

Holding On

WHEN I AM eight years old, my favorite pastime with my little brother is balancing him in the most dangerous ways on the ends of my limbs. I lie down on my back, and he climbs onto my raised feet. I flip over, he climbs on my back, and we see if he can maintain his balance while I try to stand up. We fail. Every time. And when we do, there is a lot of banging as we tumble to the floor.

One day my brother and I have come crashing down from our latest circus-like feat when my father calls us to come upstairs. We assume we are in trouble for causing so much noise. When we sit down on the bed and find out the real reason we have been summoned, we wish we had only been in trouble.

Our parents slowly explain that they will no longer be living together. They tell us that Mom is moving out. They tell us that we will stay with Dad. They tell us that we will still see Mom on a regular schedule. They tell us that we will keep going to the same school and sleep in our same beds. They assure us that they love us. They ask if we have any questions.

I'm stunned. I'd read books about this. In the books,

when a kid learns her parents are getting divorced, she is always sad and mad and disappointed and confused.

I am confused. I have never heard my parents fight or raise their voices at one another. I had no idea they were so broken. But because they present it to us as if they have everything figured out, I don't panic. I understand Mom is going to live with my grandmother. I understand that we will live with Daddy. It all sounds so simple.

Until it's not.

What I don't yet know about myself is that I live in my head. In my head I feel comfortable and safe and secure. I think a lot. I daydream a lot. I work out problems and imagine solutions. I seek to *understand* my way through the world. My parents had a plan. I understood the plan. That should have been it. But it wasn't. My emotions. My body. My heart will have some things to express, too.

The first wave of sadness finds me on August 15, 1991. It is the day my momma moves out.

When I wake up that morning, I can hear her in the kitchen. A little voice in my head whispers, *This is the last time.* This is the last morning I will wake up to the sound of her humming in our kitchen. *Our kitchen* will no longer be ours.

I roll out of bed quietly, listening to every sound she makes. The drawers creak open. The silverware inside shakes from her touch. The refrigerator door closes with a dull thud. The microwave buttons beep under her fingers.

Usually I tear down the stairs, sliding my way down the last three before catching myself at the end, sheepishly laughing that I almost wiped out . . . again. But not today. I walk slowly, deliberately. I plant every step on those stairs. I use the banister instead of sliding my hand down the wall. My little body is moving in slow motion. Grieving. And I don't know it. I am just trying to hold on to this moment that I know cannot last.

When I get to the bottom, I surprise my mom, who didn't hear me coming. "Hi, Daughter Dear," she says, looking at me intently. I watch her for a moment, before a tear slips down my face. We walk toward each other until my face is buried in her belly. I wrap my arms around her and silently beg her not to leave. *Please stay,* my little heart pleads. I don't want this to be the last time.

But I say nothing. My chest is heavy, and my mom's cotton robe is suffocating me. I move just enough to breathe. It is all I can do to breathe.

Eventually my mom pulls away. Pulls away from me. Pulls away from the house. Pulls away from our life together. But I don't remember any of that. I just remember being desperate to hold on and knowing that my little arms weren't strong enough to hold my world together.

And I remember the emptiness of our home when she is gone. Her shoes are no longer at the bottom of the closet. Her coat no longer lays across the back of the couch. Her laugh no longer fills the house. Her perfume no longer hangs in the air. Even the air itself is different because it no longer dances around the movements of her body. It's so still. The absence of her here, in our home, is palpable. And even though I still have access to her, my little body, my little heart will never be the same.

Blood

THE FIRST BIG change that happens after my mom is gone is that I get my period. I remember the first time so vividly. I was ten years old and thought I was totally prepared because Judy Blume had already told me everything I needed to know. Turns out I missed a few things.

In my Christian elementary school, we did learn about reproductive systems. I was handed a drawing and asked to point out the fallopian tubes, uterus, and vagina. I did so with flying colors. The drawing made sense enough on paper, I suppose, but I didn't fully comprehend all the ways this little drawing would have consequences and repercussions for my personal life.

There I was sitting in my classroom at ten years old when I felt the overwhelming urge to head to the bathroom. I could tell something strange was happening with my body, but I wasn't entirely sure what. It wasn't like I needed to pee, and yet my pelvic area was desperately trying to talk to me. I couldn't make out what she was saying and figured she probably wanted to talk in private.

I raised my hand and was excused with our generic hall pass—the dusty ten-inch chalkboard eraser. I was tempted to turn right out of the classroom and use the Staff Only bathroom. It was large. It had a lobby lined with comfortable couches and a wall of mirrors. It smelled good. But this was no time for sneaking around. I couldn't be on full alert until I knew what was happening with my body.

I made a left, and off to the student bathrooms I went. I was alone with my choice of the four neon-orange stalls. I slid into the middle one and stood there. Hmm. Now what? I didn't really need to go, but it seemed an appropriate place to start. I pulled off my clothes, and what did I see? A red spot in the middle of my underwear.

My period had arrived! It was wondrous. I woke up that morning ready to diagram some sentences, but I would leave school that day a new person.

Cue "I'm Every Woman."

But then I had another thought. My body was doing this on its own. Like, she didn't wait for me to get to a restroom so that my period could begin. I had misunderstood Judy Blume. I thought my period would be convenient, understanding, patient, on schedule. I thought she would wait until I needed to pee, and then appear simultaneously. Wasn't that why girls in Judy Blume books always discovered their periods in a bathroom? Big Nope. Like me, all those girls just happened to be in a bathroom when they discovered their periods had finally arrived. It waits for no one.

I snapped into action. If my period was not gonna wait for me to enter a stall, I would need something to protect my clothes for the rest of the day.

I opened my plastic Claire's purse with white and gray

stripes. All I had was the following: Two pencils. An old sticker. A tiny comb that was no match against my new growth but might straighten out my pink-roller bangs. A few pennies, nickels, and dimes in the corners. Two Jolly Ranchers—one half unwrapped and the other permanently wrapped. Lots of fuzzies.

I was not MacGyver. None of these things were going to help me today.

I looked around at the suddenly childish neon-orange walls. *Welp. Should have gone to the staff bathroom after all,* I thought. But then again, I wasn't sure my little nickels and dimes would buy me a pad from the bathroom vending machine. Did it only take quarters? I had no idea.

I turned my attention to the toilet paper roll and sighed. This was not going to be comfortable. This one-ply wonder felt more like tracing paper than cotton, but what choice did I have? I got to work folding.

Then I grabbed some more paper and kept folding. And some more. Turns out, it takes a lot of toilet paper to approximate the thickness of a pad you've only seen on a TV commercial.

As I pressed my little creation into the center of my underwear, I had another realization. Nothing was going to keep this in place. The last thing I needed was to announce my new experience to an entire classroom of friends by having a wad of maroon-stained toilet paper fall out of my pants leg. No thank you. Better wrap this little contraption into place. More toilet paper.

After pulling all my clothes into place around my invention, I felt strange . . . really strange. Strange like, my-underwear-is-stuffed-with-scratchy-toilet-paper strange. As I walked to the sink, I almost laughed at how ridiculous I felt.

Standing in front of the mirror, I tried some light calisthenics. I jogged in place. I twisted and turned. I took ridiculously long strides back and forth. I jumped up and down a couple times. I was starting to get hot, but I had to be sure this thing was not going to make a public appearance when I got up to sharpen my No. 2 pencil.

I washed my hands, threw away the brown paper towel (which felt remarkably similar to the toilet paper in my pants), grabbed the chalkboard eraser, and opened the door to the hallway. It was time to face the public.

In the classroom, I sat down uncomfortably, but proudly. It wasn't the perfect way to discover my period, but I had successfully figured out what to do on my own.

Outro: "I'm Every Woman."

. . .

OVER THE NEXT few years I learn there are lots of rules when it comes to having a period. Some of these rules—rules passed down between generations—I learn at home, but many of them I learn just by being a person who has a period in a society that would like to pretend menstruation doesn't exist.

I should tell no one. I should not talk about menstruation in public, and in private, I should call it by a euphemism only. (In our house the chosen phrase was "that time of the month," but I learned the others, too: "period," "Aunt Flow," "the crimson wave," "mother nature," "lady days," or "a visiting cousin.") I am to hide feminine products under the sink or keep them buried deep in my purse. (I have never, even now, at forty years old, seen a woman pull out a pad or tampon in mixed company and carry it to the bathroom.) I am expected to dismiss my own feelings because I must be moody and to deny the cramping and/or back pain associated with my period. I learn that menstrual blood is gross, and that seeing a used pad or tampon is disgusting. I learn that women are not supposed to talk to one another about it because no one should be able to tell that we are menstruating at all.

Even though it's natural for my preteen body to have a period, it's clear that I am supposed to pretend my body hasn't just experienced a profound change. I'm supposed to treat it like a shameful secret.

I remain deeply grateful to all the people in my life who decided to defy the rules. I am grateful to Keris, who shares about her own period pain while we sit at the lunch table. I am grateful to Brooke, who acknowledges that she is moody and then shrugs because it is what it is. I am grateful to Joy, who tells me that she hates being on her period when we have gym class, because me too. I am grateful to all the people who share about birth control and fibroids, and menstrual cups, and period underwear. I am grateful to those who defy social norms and openly discuss the pink tax and access to products. Because of these folks, I find refuge from the oppressive weight of societal denial.

And so I want to advocate for some new rules.

RULE 1: Regularly wave around tampon, pad, or whatever period product suits your fancy while loudly announcing that you need to excuse yourself to the restroom. Do this at home, at work, at the gym, while shopping in Target, doesn't matter.

RULE 2: Leave period products on an open shelf in your bathroom. First, so that everyone can clearly see them (and perhaps even purchase the correct ones when the stash is running low without having to call you twenty-seven times). Second, so we can stop contorting ourselves on the toilet while trying to reach under the sink to open the plastic tub where our products are hiding. RIDICULOUS.

RULE 3: Loudly ask in public bathrooms if anyone is in need of a pad or tampon.

RULE 4: If the dispenser is not free, leave a quarter in it for the next person's emergency.

RULE 5: Normalize mood swings by wearing T-shirts that read: YES, I AM ON MY PERIOD. YES, I AM STILL RIGHT.

RULE 6: We establish a hand signal when cramping. That hand signal means everything stops so that a woman can speak. I need the amount of cramping our bodies are doing to equal the amount of space our voices take up in the room. If we must endure this pain outside of our homes, I demand that it be worth our time.

RULE 7: We must band together to curse anyone who is dismissive of us because we are "PMSing." Place "Curse" on business cards and stickers for easy reciting:

Woe to the humans
who condescendingly mouth
PMSing,
who dismiss femininity
and twist masculinity
to uphold inequality
on broken stilts of mediocrity.
May the expression of our emotion
be the start of your demotion,
breaking opportunity
to define our reality.
We predict a power failure
that sets us free.
And when you lie in bed wondering
how this came to be,
may you recollect
me.

Carry

I COULD TALK to my dad about almost anything when I was a kid. While there were certainly things I kept to myself, I was nonetheless able to tell him about crushes and school drama. I was able to ask him questions about the divorce and anything about my parents' past. The only time I remember my dad being stunned by one of my revelations is when I announced that I had gotten my period.

When I heard him and my stepmom bustling around the kitchen that evening, I decided to make my entrance. I often talked to him while he cooked. All the movement somehow made my confessions less awkward.

When I made my announcement, "Daddy. Ummm. I got my period today," all the movement, all the sound in the kitchen stopped. I could swear even the water stopped boiling.

"What?" he asked, eyes wide, mouth hanging slightly open. This is my father's please-tell-me-I-misheard-you face.

I repeated quietly, "I got my period today."

My dad turned to face my stepmom. She looked back at him. Not a word was exchanged, but a lot was said. Neither spoke for a few seconds as they resumed cooking.

I waited.

Finally, my dad spoke over his shoulder as he chopped something on the counter. "Okay. June is going to show you what to do. Go ahead to the bathroom."

Standing in front of the sink, she showed me how to unwrap a pad and put it in my panties. "When you've finished with a pad, this is how you throw it away." She demonstrated. *Oh my goodness,* I thought to myself. *This is why there are little garbage cans attached to the walls of public bathrooms.* It was all making sense.

Then came a somber talk about womanhood.

"Austin. Men are going to be interested in you. And now that you have your period, you can get pregnant. You must guard yourself." I think there was more after that, but my mind was reeling. This was not what happened in Judy Blume books.

The hushed tones. The whispered instructions. The energy of the entire house shifted. The warnings felt ominous. Inevitable.

What does it mean that men will be interested in me? Which men? Like, grown men, or is "men" a stand-in for "boys"? How do I guard myself? I'm ten years old. I'm not going to get pregnant, am I? I nod fervently when I think I'm supposed to. My discomfort grows under the weight of questions I'm not sure I want the answers to. I start feeling claustrophobic in this small room with the door closed. I am desperate to leave this energy of pure fear . . . and sadness. I am so struck by the sadness.

I would soon learn, she wasn't wrong to warn me.

When I am eleven years old, my mom gets a new boyfriend. Men are always interested in her. At the grocery store. Walking down the sidewalk. Standing in lines. At one point I'm certain even her white minister has a crush on her. She is pretty and smart and charming and has a big ole butt. Men are always tripping over themselves to get to her.

But for the moment, she is dating Anthony.

Anthony is the son of a woman who also attends our church, and he has a daughter even younger than me. Anthony is funny and he's handy. He helps my mom fix plumbing, paint walls, and move furniture in her new house. I do not live with my mom, so I appreciate that he is helpful to her. It makes me feel like someone is looking out for her.

But I am also afraid to be left alone with him.

One day, Anthony comes over when my mom isn't home. I let him into our breezeway, a covered space that connects the garage to the side door of the house. He stands in the doorway as I look down on him from the top of four steps. There are probably two feet between us. I can smell the cigarette he just finished smoking, but it's mixed with something else. The smell is stronger every time he opens his mouth to speak. I think it might be alcohol.

I don't know much about these things, as my own parents don't drink with any regularity, but I once overheard my grandmother whisper a warning to my mom. She said that Anthony had come over that day and she could smell the liquor on his breath. "Be careful," she said, placing a hand on my mom's shoulder. I wasn't supposed to hear that, but I felt a sense of validation when I did. Her warning affirmed that the danger I sometimes felt around him wasn't made up in my head. And now, as he slouches in the doorway, trying to focus on me, I suspect that more than a cigarette is influencing this moment.

Anthony talks to me and asks questions about Mom. But in the middle of the conversation, he tells me how pretty I am. How I am his favorite girl. He asks if I'm going to give him a hug.

And it feels wrong. His glassy eyes burn through me, but he doesn't seem to be listening to anything I'm saying. I know when I am being purposefully charming, and I am not saying or doing anything that would warrant this kind of praise. Are his eyes dropping to my shirt . . . my shorts . . . my legs? I take a step backwards, but I also laugh, pretending to delight in his attention. He reaches to hold on to the banister inside the house, placing one foot on the bottom step.

I have no chance of closing the door now. My head is telling me everything is fine; that I know Anthony, that he wouldn't hurt me. But my body is unconvinced. It's confusing, because I'm glad my mom has Anthony, and he has never been mean, yet I don't like the way I feel when I'm alone with him.

Just seconds later, my little brother pulls himself away from the TV and joins us. I don't know if he could hear my concern telepathically, but I am glad he has entered the room. Eric takes over the conversation, and eventually Anthony looks bored. He slides back from the doorway, and I can finally take a deep breath . . . a breath I didn't know I was holding.

He saunters back to his car and waves goodbye. He tells us to let Mom know he stopped by. We promise.

As I shut the door, I feel a wave of relief that I don't have language for. So, I just follow my brother into the next room and watch him watch TV, waiting for the coldness to leave my body.

It will not be the last time I have this sensation of danger, of being watched. I feel it again when I am catcalled by men standing outside corner stores and gas stations. I feel it when men holler at me or whistle from their cars. I feel it on my college campus and sometimes at the club. I feel it at church from time to time. I once felt it in my home when I invited a coworker to stop by and quickly discovered he had very specific assumptions about the invitation. It's a tingling in my brain, a sensation that rings *danger*.

As I get older I learn how to protect myself against this fear. Carry keys between your fingers. Carry quarters to call a cab. Carry a cell to call for help. Carry pepper spray. Carry yourself with modesty. It's this last one that offers more harm than protection.

Thanks to the unique mix that was my Christian school, Black church, and religious home, I earn the equivalent of a doctoral degree in "womanly modesty." It involved uniforms, lap scarves, and raising my arms over my head to make sure my clothes are not too short. It involved taming my ambition and my sexuality, warning me at sixteen that if I have sex with my boyfriend, Satan will make sure I get pregnant. It will be years before I learn to recognize the ways modesty is wielded as a form of control.

Everywhere I turn, adults seem convinced that I have control. That I can control other people knowing when I'm on my period. That I can control avoiding the freshman fifteen. That I can control getting pregnant. That I can control how men think about my body. That I can control how school administrators think about my body. That I can control how white people think about my body. What takes me longer to unlearn, what I am still unlearning now, is how little of my body I control in the first place.

From the first moment my period arrives in the middle of class, my body is revealing a lesson altogether different. My body is largely unconcerned about my ability to exert control over it. Instead, it wants me to be attentive to it. My mom is the first person to show me how.

Agency

MY MOM AND dad have vastly different reactions to my revelation that my period has started. I don't remember the exact moment I told my mom; I suspect I called her. But I vividly remember her reaction the next time I visited her.

She walks into the bathroom and opens the cabinet doors below the sink. There she has a ministore of menstruation products. She pulls out the boxes of pads first. "Okay, here are the ones I wear when my period is heavy." She hands me a bulky wad of plastic. "And these are the ones I wear when my period is starting to wane." She hands me a thinner one, called a "panty liner." "Then I also have these, which I sometimes wear at night because my period gets unruly and can destroy my panties." She unwraps that pad so I can fully see how it's different from the others. It covers almost the entire buttocks! I put it on my underwear.

"Oh, I like this," I tell her.

She laughs. "Why do you like this one?" she asks, genuinely curious as to why I would choose the biggest one.

"Because it covers everything," I blurt. At that point I still have big worries about leaks and showing. I don't know how heavy my period is going to be, and this pad is basically a thin diaper, offering guaranteed protection. (I would wear it maybe two more times and never reach for it again. Too much, turns out.)

I see another pink box under the sink. "What are those?" I ask.

"Those are called 'tampons,'" she replies.

I've seen commercials for tampons. They soak up blue liquid. But I am unclear about how that little contraption could protect my undies and my dignity.

"You wanna try it?" she asks.

"Sure," I say, eyeing it suspiciously as she throws away the plastic cover.

She tells me to lay back on the bed. "Okay, you're going to put this end in the hole where your period comes out," she instructs.

That sounds easy enough, until it dawns on me that I am not sure which hole my period comes out from. I assumed my period was passing through the same place where I urinate. But no. There is an additional hole down here that I have never noticed! Wait . . . was this on the diagram of my reproductive organs?

My eyes are wide with wonder. Three holes. Who knew? As I continue trying to insert the tampon, I keep asking her, "Is this the right hole? I can't see." She's laughing so hard at the number of times I have said "hole" that her eyes are filling with tears. After multiple hesitant tries, eventually I get it right and stand up. "Okay!" she chirps. "How does that feel?"

"Weird!" I respond honestly, my face all scrunched up. "I feel all . . . plugged up."

She laughs again. And I can't help giggling, too. "Well, that's kind of what you want. You want it to catch your period. And when you're finished with it, you pull this string to get it out." I was, at that moment, trying to ignore the string. It was tickling my thigh, reminding me of the plastic plugging the hole I never knew I'd had.

I look at my mom, overwhelmed by all the sensations. "I don't think I like this," I say, shaking my head.

"That's okay. You can use pads for now, and when you're ready we can always try the tampon again."

Before we move on with the rest of our day, my mom places her hands on my shoulders. "If you ever have questions about any of this, you know you can always talk to me, right? I will always tell you the truth."

"I know, Momma," I said, "I know."

I am grateful for the ways she teaches me to practice agency—to decide what I am comfortable with and to know I can try something new on my own time line. I am grateful for her openness. And yet, there are still some things about my body I tell no one.

Allergies

WHEN I WAS around eleven or twelve, my mother finally gave in to my pleading to get my ears pierced. But she had a warning on the way to the mall: "Austin, you might be allergic to earrings, like I am."

I was desperate for her to be wrong, but of course she was right. Not long after I had the earrings in, my ear lobes turned itchy, then blistery, then crusty. Even now, I better not keep earrings in for more than two hours, no matter how "hypoallergenic" they are.

What took me far longer to understand is that I don't have an ear allergy, I have a *skin* allergy. My neck is allergic to necklaces. My fingers are allergic to rings. My belly is allergic to belt buckles. But nothing shocked me more than discovering my armpits are allergic to deodorant, which is deeply problematic for a girl entering puberty.

With puberty comes a reality that adults in my life called "mustiness." Musty is different from sweaty or dirty. It sneaks up on me. Musty happens when my temperature temporarily rises at the spicy paragraph in the novel I'm reading. Musty happens when I'm bent over the bathtub to clean the ring of dirt, but all I can smell is Comet. Musty happens when

I climb two flights of stairs still wearing the hoodie that kept me warm outside.

I am warned that it's important I start wearing deodorant. But deodorant hurts. It begins with the same itching I experience anytime metal touches my body. It is an itch that takes all the focus away from what is happening around me. An itch that screams and refuses to disappear. An itch that feels better when I scratch—not because the itching stops, but because then only pain is left.

Scratching my armpits requires some very delicate moves. It's not like I can just raise my arm in the middle of class and start scraping my armpit. That's not normal. So I have to develop other ways to make it happen. My first move is to pretend I have an itch on my shoulder, but while scratching it, I tuck my thumb under my armpit, where it can do God's true work. The other move is to fold both arms across my chest, like I'm giving myself a hug, and scratch both underarms that way.

Either way, clawing at myself makes things worse. The next time I put on deodorant, it won't just itch, it will sting and then burn. There is a constant level of desperation I have to ignore every day, because all I want is to grab a cold towel and wipe it all off. Just erase the decision to wear it and hope the coolness will counter the burning. But I can't. I have to wear the deodorant, because I am musty. And sometimes dirty or sweaty, too. And so I curl my toes and wait for the stinging to end, the burning to transition back to itching, and the cycle begins again and again and again.

It isn't long before my rashes develop blisters. And the blisters create pus. And when I scratch at those blisters, the pus turns to blood. All of it turns into scars. My underarms are dark with scar tissue.

By junior high, I can't do it anymore; I can't wear deodorant every day. I begin every morning employing a complicated equation. I must consider weather, the material of my shirt, and the physicality expected of me that day. Every day is lose-lose, regardless of my decision. Every day that I wear deodorant, I am embarrassed and ashamed of my secret desire to rip my own armpits off. When I don't, I walk past my friends, my teachers, my crush, wondering how bad I smell.

I am afraid that my body is offensive to everyone around me. I wonder if they are embarrassed of me . . . or for me. And, as I soon discover, at least one person is.

Punishment

IN THE WAKE of my parents' divorce, destabilization continues to ripple through my life. Babysitters come and go. My parents date other people, break up with other people, marry other people, divorce other people. The number of adults in my life who have some sense of authority over me without really knowing me is constantly in flux. Some of them love me. Some of them are annoyed by me. Some of them ignore me. It is always changing, and I simply hang on as best I can.

Among all these people, there is one who comes into my life when I am musty. And my fickle relationship with deodorant drives her crazy. She has no idea that deodorant is difficult for me to wear. Since I can't always smell my own mustiness, I've failed at hiding my avoidance of deodorant more often than I've realized. And one day, she has had it.

After school she informs me that I will be learning how to take a shower that day. I honestly hadn't thought there was more to it than turning on the water, soaping up a towel to rub over my body, and rinsing off. No one told me there were more steps.

"You're going to learn right now," she says. She follows me into the bathroom and starts giving orders. "Take off your clothes. Turn on the shower. Get in." Her voice is hard and sharp. I feel like I'm standing on the edge of it and one wrong move will slice me open.

I climb in and start to close the frosted glass door. "No, keep it open," she says.

For a moment I am frozen. I can hardly look at her, and yet I am desperate to believe she did not just say that.

I keep my hand on the door a moment longer, trying to breathe. My brain is screaming, *She is going to watch me completely naked. She is going to watch me completely naked.* The humiliation I feel in this moment is unbearable. All I can do is confirm that it's really happening.

I hazard a glance in her direction. Her unyielding glare answers my question. This is really happening.

As I lather soap onto my body, she watches and critiques.

"Make the water hotter. It's not hot enough."

I turn the water up.

"Get more soap."

I lather again.

"Don't miss that spot."

I wipe an additional time.

"Make the water hotter, Austin."

I already can't stand under the water; it's already too hot. But I obey and turn the knob again. I stand mostly out of the spray's direct path. As a result, my wet body is freezing. I wash every goosebump as quickly as I can.

"Get your underarms again."

I wipe as gingerly as I can while pretending to scrub. I cannot scrub my blistered skin.

"Turn up the water," she repeats.

The water is too hot. Even with the steam filling up the bathroom, I am so cold.

I know there is one more body part, but I really don't want to wash my private area in front of her . . . in front of anyone. I don't want to do *any* of this in front of anyone. I reach to turn the water off.

"No, you have to get your private area."

For the first time since I turned the faucet on, I look over at her instead of straight ahead into the water. I try to hold back tears.

"Let's go," she says.

I squat a little, spreading my feet apart and gently wipe. "No. Scrub harder." So, I do. "No. Scrub harder," she repeats. Her voice grows louder. "Scrub harder, Austin. You need to get yourself clean. Is that water hot? You need to get clean."

I take two steps forward into the hot water. It stings, but it also conceals the tears streaming down my face. I am shivering. My body is stunned from having gone from the cold air to the heat of the water now coursing down my torso, stabbing my feet like pins. All I remember is shivering and then shuddering and then shivering again. Heat rises around me and my body is still shivering.

In this moment, I cannot make a distinction between the burn of the hot water and the ache of my visceral pain. I have a deep desire to separate from my body—to feel nothing. I do not want to feel the water. I do not want to feel the hardness of the tub under my feet. I do not want to feel the soapy washcloth in my hand. I do not want to feel someone's eyes on me. I do not want to feel. I am desperate to escape my body and my shame of being trapped, naked in the bathroom. By the time I am allowed to step out of the shower, my mortification has doubled back over on itself, arriving at numb.

I didn't learn how to properly take a shower that day. I learned how to fear showers.

I learned to hate the cold feeling that washes over all of us when we turn the water off and open the door. I learned that the cold feeling is dangerous and the only way to avoid the cold feeling is to not take a shower at all. I learned that shower stalls specifically and that bathrooms more broadly are not safe places. I learned that my most private area is dirty and in need of scrubbing . . . hard. I learned that my body is dirty. Not that it sometimes becomes dirty. I learned that it *is* dirty.

And I am ashamed of it. I am ashamed that I cannot control my allergies, my mustiness, my smell, or my privacy.

For years after this, my body is a nuisance to me. I do not enjoy taking care of it. I do not enjoy showering. I do not enjoy shaving. I do not enjoy putting on lotion. I do not enjoy washing my hair or wearing perfume. I do not enjoy spa treatments. My only indulgence is elaborately painting my nails. Looking back, I see that I placed all the care I wished I could have given to my whole body on that tiny real estate of my being.

The first time I am snapped out of being able to mostly pretend I am just a walking brain is pregnancy. With pregnancy comes a profound degree of embodiment. I cannot escape my body. I cannot ignore my body. I have to sink into it.

Expecting

I LOVED BEING pregnant with my son. We conceived on purpose, but it did not happen immediately, as I was led to believe it would. It took quite some time, actually. Turns out I was not destined to get pregnant the first time I had sex, as I had been warned over and over again. I also didn't get pregnant the second, third, or fourth time. It had been drilled into me that my body would simply conceive without much effort. Conceiving wasn't at all in my control.

I loved being pregnant with my son. We conceived on purpose. But I did not enjoy the experience of pregnancy. I did not enjoy the relentless vomiting. I did not enjoy that I could not control if the baby kicked my bladder or pinched a nerve in my back or slept while I was awake and was awake while I attempted to sleep. I did not enjoy being poked and prodded internally so doctors could analyze changes that were invisible to me. And I could control none of it.

I loved being pregnant with my son. We conceived on purpose. But never have I felt more responsible for my body and yet so useless. I could not will my body to grow his lungs. I could not command my body to make his heart start beating. I could not decide that today would be the day I'd create a toe or fire the synapses in his developing brain. I could not convince him to grow, to turn over, to cooperate for an ultrasound. Every week, doctors asked me a million questions that all seemed to imply that I was in control, and yet all I could do was exist as best I could. Everyone asks *How are you?* and *How is the baby?* But I could never answer the second question. I had no idea. I was not in control of how or when this baby would show up in the world. We were one body, and we were not.

I loved being pregnant with my son. We conceived on purpose. And it is still the hardest thing I have ever asked my body and my emotions to endure, because after all the mythmaking about my body, it turned out I have rarely been in control of it.

I couldn't control pregnancy. I couldn't control labor. I have never been in control of how men process my body, regardless of what I'm wearing. I have never been in control of how the church processes my body, no matter how I tried to stay covered. I have never been in control of how schools process my body, in uniform or out of it. I have never been in control of how the workplace processes my body, regardless of my relaxed hair or swapping out my contacts for glasses. I have never been in control of how society processes my body as a Black woman. It turns out the only thing I can control, I had to learn to do myself: and that is to love my body.

I had to love it through pregnancy. I had to love it through labor. I had to love it through postpartum. I have to love it as my weight cycles. I have to love it as it keeps changing. I have to choose love every day.

By love, I do not mean that I am always satisfied with exactly what my body is experiencing. I do not mean that I look in the mirror and am forever pleased. It has more to do with how I treat my body than with how I feel about it.

I did not enjoy pregnancy, but I still took the iron pills when I felt I could keep them down, because I chose to give love to my body. I did not enjoy pregnancy, but I still stayed away from the laundry list of foods I could not consume safely, because that was how I could choose love. I don't always love my size, but I choose to give my body love by putting on clothes that make me feel good or warm or cozy or sexy or calm or powerful. Even with all the options of aluminum-free deodorant, I still struggle to find the one that won't make me itch, but I keep trying new brands because my body is worth that effort. And sometimes I love her by not wearing any at all in the safety of my home, and apologize with vulnerability to my family who understand.

I don't always feel a sense of love. But I am learning to give it, because that is what I can actually control.

Contractions

I WOKE UP at 2:00 A.M., my core twisting in on itself. The day before, I'd had an appointment with my ob-gyn, who told me I'd started dilating. She was quick to add that it could still be a few more days before baby arrives. But this morning my body is saying, *Not so much*.

I quietly climb out of the bed because something feels different. I am cramping a bit—a sensation I haven't felt since my period disappeared. I gently shake my husband awake. "Babe, it might not be time just yet—" My sentence is interrupted by what feels like another cramp. When it is gone, it's like nothing happened. I continue telling my husband that today might be the day.

Tommie, possessing zero chill, leaps out of bed. He races to the bathroom to put in his contacts while he calls the hospital. "We just want to let you know we are on our way," he declares into the speakerphone with one finger in his eye.

The nurse who answers has a few questions to ask before we make the decision to hop in the car. Tommie is not on board with her assessment. "Okay! We are on our way," he keeps replying after answering each question. She quickly figures out we must be first-time parents and welcomes us to come over, as long as we understand she might send us back home depending on how things progress.

Another contraction. I place both hands on the bed and wait for him to hang up.

He shoves his contacts into his eyes, grabs our bags, and we are out the door.

The car ride is fifteen minutes.

"You okay?" Tommie asks.

"Yeah, I'm here, babe."

"All right, we are gonna get you to the hospital and get you all checked in."

"I know you will."

We are quiet for a moment. The weight of what's happening is equal parts heavy and elating. We both reach toward the armrest and clasp hands, the city lights bright in the night.

I break the silence. "You know, honey . . . I'm a little scared. I read everything I could about labor and delivery. But the one thing I could not handle were all the terrible stories and statistics connected to the mortality rates of Black women."

"I guess we should talk about this hospital, huh?" he asks in reply.

"Yeah," I whisper, even though it's just the two of us. "I think we need a plan if something goes wrong and the doctors aren't listening to me."

"You're right," he says. He leans forward in the driver's seat while thinking. "What we'll do is make it clear that I'm an attorney. That's all we'll say, we won't tell them what kind of attorney."

"Oh, that's good. We don't have to tell them it's for juveniles," I half smile.

Over the next two hours at the hospital, the contractions slowly grow stronger, coming faster and harder. Just when a contraction blows through my body so hard two people have to keep me from falling, an epidural arrives. The anesthesiologist is my new best friend. Within minutes, my whole body calms down.

I lay back in the bed, feeling exhausted from the contractions. Then I notice I can't feel anything. I can't feel my legs. I can't feel a single contraction. I am shaking in my bed, like shivers that don't subside. My jaw keeps locking so I can't speak. I can't tell anyone that I don't feel much of anything.

Unexpectedly a machine next to me starts beeping. The nurse rushes back into our room. She is harried, but her voice is calm. "Hi, Mom. Looks like your blood pressure is dropping pretty low, and baby's is following. So we are going to take a look, okay?" All I can do is stare back at her. She turns to address Tommie. "Hey, Dad, four more doctors are going to join me in here. Don't be alarmed, we all have a different job to make sure your wife and baby are okay."

This is what we dreaded. Something has gone wrong, but I can't speak. I can't advocate for myself at all. I'm staring at Tommie, praying that the calmness of the nurse is indicative of the care my body will receive. Before I can finish my prayer, everything goes dark.

When I awake I am tired, as if I haven't been knocked out for an hour, but I'm fine. When my husband sees my eyes are open, we hold one another's gaze and whisper "Hi." Still here. Still in labor.

We didn't need to employ our plan, but we are a little overwhelmed that we had one and couldn't use it. We hope this is evidence that we won't need it.

Four hours later, baby is born and we are both healthy. But that never for a moment felt like a guarantee.

Postpartum

AT HEART, I am a researcher. Not the academic kind, the anxious kind. Researching calms me. Before cooking a new dish, I read five different versions of the recipe (and the first page of reviews on all five). Before writing, I read about writing. And you better believe that when I got pregnant, the first thing I did was march myself to the nearest bookstore to buy half of the what-to-expect-when-you're-expecting section. I went to classes. I asked questions from the other new parents around me.

I tried hard to resist using the internet this time, because I quickly found it to be filled with the worst possible stories about labor, and that was not what my anxiety needed. I'm a Black woman in the United States, where the mortality rate while giving birth is two to three times higher for me than it is for white women. The possibility of racism killing me was plenty scary. I didn't need more reasons to worry. So, I consumed books, lectures, conversations, and phone apps that helped explain what my body was doing and why. I was on a hunt to feel prepared.

Most of what I read landed in one of three sections:

This is how your body changes during pregnancy.
This is how you get through labor.
This is how you care for a newborn.

In hindsight, the part none of them covered as explicitly as I wished was what happens to my body after labor.

Only one person (a new mom herself) broached the subject candidly. My friend Rachel sent me an email that began "Austin, I know preparing for a new baby is overwhelming. So I hope this email isn't. I wanted to send you a list of some items that were very helpful to me after my labor." And what followed was a list, including links, of the things she purchased to help her postpartum body. It was my only window into what was about to happen. God bless you, Rach.

The following is my adaptation of Rachel's email. It is my manifesto, my mission to have no one ever be in the dark about the hellscape that is recovering from your body being ripped apart as a whole human escapes from its embrace. This matters to me because this was the season when I had to love my body more intentionally than I ever had before. I could not coast through this recovery. My body was changing fast and in profound ways. She would not be ignored, so I had to be attentive to her. And I want everyone to have what they need to take care of their own sacred selves . . . especially when things get messy. And everything gets messy.

(The following describes a postvaginal birth. I would make another list for those who endure a C-section, but I haven't had that experience. Nonetheless, I hope there is some information here that will be of help.)

Dear Person I Love,

I know you have been eagerly awaiting the birth of your child. Your registry is probably filled with baby clothes and bottle warmers and books and toys and diapers. But there are some people who are going to buy things for *you* . . . these people are the best. Keep them around. They are likely to buy you something whimsical like luxurious bubble bath or the candles that make a sound like a crackling fire. Tell them the following is what you *really* need. Add these items to your registry. Make a list at Target or Walmart or wherever people will whip out a credit card. This is not the time to be shy. Get what you need, honey! Here is a list to get you started, whether you add it to your registry or pick it up on your own:

1. Perineal ice packs. You're gonna learn a lot about your perineum, but for now you just need to know that these ice packs are for your vag. If you get an epidural, you may not need them right away, but Good Lord, have them on standby. If you have a vaginal birth, steal as many as you can from the hospital (think looting). Even with my stolen bag of them, I still used every single one in the box I purchased online. Yes, a box. Now, I have read that

you can make them yourself, but please believe you'll have enough going on without worrying about the DYI ice pack in your underwear melting, okay? Only scientists know what is still coming out of your body, and your baby is still pooping black ink. So, give yourself a break. These only require a snap, a shake, and instant relief!

2. Underwear for incontinence. This section is your friend. Claim the space. Stand there with pride. These special undergarments are going to be your friends. They are soft. They cover all the things. You don't have to worry about all the juices leaving your body ruining them. Now, the ones I went for had a cute little bow design. I know it sounds silly, but that bow did a lot of emotional heavy lifting when my vag hurt and my breasts were leaking and tears were being shed. That tiny little bow reminded me of the part of myself that was quickly being lost—the part that enjoys delicate, pretty things and yelled a lot fewer cusswords.

3. Extra-large, supersize pads. Preferably, you want the kind that stretch from the small of your back to your belly button. Whatever size those are, buy them. Your first two periods might be a little overwhelming . . . and you may not be ready for a tampon quite so soon.

4. A laxative and poo softener. My very first poo after giving birth was fine. The epidural was

still wearing off and it felt almost normal. The next one, however . . . I almost cracked the toilet seat from gripping so hard. I was doing that thing where I wasn't even completely sitting on the toilet seat anymore because my toes were curling and I desperately wanted to separate from my body and somehow my brain thought, *Maybe if I half stand up, gravity will be more potent and help this process.* I don't know, it's hard to explain. The point is, buy the stool softener. Use the stool softener. Thank the heavens for the stool softener. And if you find that you become constipated, use a laxative-softener combo. You'll thank me when it's all over.

5. Nursing pads for your breasts. Get a big box, chil'. When my milk first came in, my body felt tingly, but my body was feeling so many things, I didn't give it a second thought. Until ten minutes later, when I moved and discovered my milk had soaked my shirt, my pillow, and the bedsheets I was laying on. Dammit. After that, I used these on a very regular basis.

6. All things nipples: I did use a cold/hot pack for my breasts. Cold when they were in pain from breast-feeding and warm when my milk was coming in and they hurt. Putting the warmth on them helped the milk come down for baby or pumping. I also used a nipple guard because I knew I wasn't going to nurse for long. It made feeding my child

bearable and then pleasant especially when my nipples were sore and sensitive. I also loved the Soothies cooling pads. Sometimes the ice packs were too cold, but the Soothies were always perfect.

7.   Take everything the hospital offers. Don't be shy. The two things I used the most (other than the vagina ice packs) were the peri bottle and the Dermoplast spray. When you first start peeing again, wiping is not going to be your initial instinct. You are going be your own bidet by using that peri bottle to gently wash (please be mindful of the temp of the water in said peri bottle). After washing, there is the spraying of the Dermoplast. Okay, so you know how sometimes when you cut yourself there is pain, but then as it heals there is soreness and itching and burning? Same. Same. The Dermoplast spray makes things more comfortable as you heal. The hospital also provided extra-strength painkillers. Take the painkillers. I did not know that my uterus would not just quickly return to size postbaby but that it would *cramp* back to its normal size. The one time I forgot to take the medicine on schedule, I could not move. I was sitting in a rocking chair, perfectly still, when my mom noticed tears streaming down my face. I could hardly speak. I squeaked out, "Motrin. Forgot Motrin," and she went arunning. Anyway, my point is, if the hospital offers it, take it. And if the hospital doesn't offer it, ask for it.

8. I needed options for hemorrhoids because pushing a baby out causes hemorrhoids that are about 1000 percent bigger than the ones that come from constipation. Tucks pads and hemorrhoid cream were both necessities.

9. A basket. You're going to put all of this in a little basket. The function of the basket is not to pretend we are organizing for a show on HGTV. You need a basket because every item on this list needs to be contained in one place. If the basket is out of reach and you need the Dermoplast spray, I want you to be able to yell to anyone in earshot, "I need my basket! Someone get my basket." Imagine for a moment that you sent someone to get the Dermoplast spray and they came back with a peri bottle . . . you might have to kill that person, and that would be so unfortunate during this beautiful time of welcoming a new life into your home.

10. Bubble bath and candles. Why not if you're into that kind of thing?

So that's the email. I would like to conclude by acknowledging that embodiment isn't always pretty. It's not always adornment and style and lotions and potions that make us feel special. Sometimes embodiment is gross and painful and itchy and dripping. I believe with my whole heart that our care for ourselves when our bodies are messy matters deeply.

I Love Myself When
I Am Falling Apart

Caring for myself is not
self-indulgence, it is self-
preservation, and that is
an act of political warfare.

—AUDRE LORDE,
A Burst of Light

Chronic

IN AN ATTEMPT to be grown-ups, my husband and I decide it's time for us to increase our life insurance policies and create wills. We are parents now and want to make sure our son will be cared for should anything happen to us. My father is an insurance agent, so he walks us through the paperwork to get things started.

Once the paperwork is submitted, my father gives me a call. "Austin," he says, "because you are considered overweight, someone is going to come by your house to give you a short physical."

It's annoying but fine, especially since I don't have to go to the doctor's office. A young white woman comes to our home. She takes my blood pressure, sticks me with a needle, and has me pee into a cup. It takes ten minutes and she is back in her car.

Four days later, my father calls again. "Austin, I need you to get a full physical done," he says. He then tells me I have been denied a life insurance increase, because the numbers from my urine analysis are off. I am stunned. "They won't give me additional details beyond this," my dad tells me, "including the actual numbers. So I need you to get checked out. In the meantime, I'll work on this."

When I hang up the phone I just sit on the edge of my bed. *I have been denied a life insurance increase because it's too likely I'll actually die?* "What is happening?" I say out loud, to no one.

I get my bloodwork done again, and when I get the results, I google the words I don't understand, which is all of them. Once I have sufficiently freaked myself out, I call my doctor. She says, "Sometimes bodies are weird. Let's run the numbers one more time, and I'll set you up with a nephrologist, a kidney doctor, just in case."

After taking these tests three more times, I'm sitting in a doctor's office, watching the face of a nephrologist, searching it for clues about my situation. She analyzes the numbers on her computer screen and says "huh" over and over again. When she turns back to me, I'm hoping for answers, but all she has is questions for me.

"Have you ever had issues with your kidneys before?"

"I don't think so," I reply.

"Do your parents have issues with their kidneys?"

"I don't think so," I reply.

"Have you ever been injured—kicked or taken a fall— that could have injured your kidneys?"

"I don't think so," I reply again, then add, "Where would an injury have to have taken place in order to impact my kidneys?"

She blinks at me.

"I don't know where my kidneys are," I explain.

She smiles, crossing the room toward me. She gently

rubs my back. "They are here and here," she says. She continues to stand next to me while I consider the question. Could I have injured my kidneys and not known it? Did I forget about a time I was drop-kicked in the back? Have I ever fallen so hard on ice or snow that my internal organs could have been damaged?

I sigh and tell her that the most violent thing my body has ever endured is pregnancy and labor.

She has a few more questions. She is searching for a reason why someone my age would be having kidney problems. In the end, she decides I should get an ultrasound. She hopes it might shed some light on the situation.

The ultrasound technician is pleasantly chatty without overwhelming me. The gel she must use is cold, but that is the least of my worries in this moment. For this scan I have to lay on my side, which means I can see the screen as she runs the device over my back. My kidneys light up in neon green and blue. I have only ever had an ultrasound for my baby, but I instinctively know that healthy kidneys aren't two colors. She continues to chat with me. Her joviality keeps me from panicking as I roll over, now away from the screen, so she can scan the other kidney.

Once I've wiped off all the gel and she flicks on the overhead lights, she can clearly read the distress written all over my face. She lays a hand on my arm and says, "I'm going to put a rush on these, okay?" I look into her green eyes and thank her, hoping she understands the depth of my gratitude for being so gentle with me.

Back in the doctor's office the next day, my nephrologist looks over the scans. "You definitely have chronic kidney disease," she states before telling me a little more about the numbers and the scans. All I hear is that I have a chronic condition. A few weeks ago, I was just trying to increase my life insurance policy. Now I am being told that my kidneys will *never* fully function the way they should. I'm over-whelmed. I skim all the posters hanging on her office walls. The stages of kidney disease. The importance of dialysis. Suggestions for diet. My head is swimming. How is this possible? I'm in my thirties. *What is happening?*

I'm snapped back into the moment when I hear her say the word "biopsy." I'm young, and she can't figure out why my kidneys are damaged. I am not a smoker. I rarely drink. We already covered injuries. She wants to determine the ex-tent of the damage and maybe the cause.

I call my husband as soon as I leave her office building. "Just come on home, babe," he says tenderly. I climb into my car, and for a second I have forgotten how to turn it on. "Focus, Austin, focus," I say out loud. I know how to get home, but I turn on my GPS anyway. I don't trust myself not to get lost.

When I pull into my driveway, I call my mom. Then my mentor. Then my friends. By the time I tell my friends, I can no longer hold it together. I croak out that it's been con-firmed that I have chronic kidney disease and now I need to get a biopsy done.

My friends come to me. They drop everything and

spend the weekend with me. They cuddle me. They play with my son. They feed me and my family. They are fully and totally present to me and my fear. They hold me up when I am drowning in a sea of what-ifs. They come to me when I don't understand what is happening to my body. When I can't stop it. Or reverse it. Or change it. They come and make me stronger.

Biopsy

THEN IT'S TIME. I'm off to the hospital for a biopsy, in which the doctors will push a needle through my lower back and remove a piece of my kidney to study. It's an overnight stay, but not in a private room. All of us who've had minimally invasive procedures done are lined up in two rows against the walls, separated only by heavy gray curtains. We cannot see one another, but we can hear everything. And because this is still during the Covid era, we are all on our own.

I can hear other patients talking to their doctors about their bodies. I am not supposed to get up, not even to pee. But there is one situation I overhear that tests my resolve.

I try to pass the time away by watching TV on my iPad. I'm deep into a show I love, and the new season has just been released. I'm bingeing episodes when I hear a Black woman begin to cry, "You're not listening to me." I take out my earbuds. "This is really painful," she says. "My breast hurts so much. And my doctor said that you should drain it and prescribe something new." Her voice rises in desperation. I can tell she has already said these words a couple times by the measure in her voice.

I pause my show, trying to peek around the corner of

my curtain. I get just a glimpse of a Black woman in dark gray sweats doubled over in pain. Her long nails clutch her breast, tenderly cradling it while her other hand gestures at a white woman standing in front of her. The white woman explains that they are going to give her some pills, an antibiotic of some kind, and send her home.

"No," she says forcefully through tears. "That is not going to work. I have already been on those pills, but here I am back again. Please give me the treatment I am requesting. I need intravenous medication to resolve this." The white woman is irritated. Her voice is tense as she declares evenly, "I am not going to do that."

The Black woman is reaching for a viable solution. "Fine," she says, "then let me go through surgery again." The white woman refuses to approve the procedure. "You have two options," she states. "Take the pills or nothing." The Black woman responds over and over again, "You're not listening. You're not listening. Why won't you listen to me?"

The whole time, I am debating if I should risk my own health to get up and help advocate for her. She is alone because of Covid. I know I shouldn't stand, but I might be the only other Black woman who can hear what's going on. I cannot see her very well, but I understand her. I believe her. I'm trying to determine what I should do.

I can hear the white woman spin on her heels and march down the makeshift hallway, her shoes flapping against the shiny linoleum floor as she walks away. The Black woman picks up her cellphone. It sounds like she's talking to her partner, so I stay put. She is sobbing about being in pain and repeating what the doctor told her. She calms as she listens to the voice on the other end.

When the doctor appears again, the Black woman continues her plea for intravenous medication. And again, the doctor is becoming increasingly annoyed. I can hear the Black woman sob before taking another trembling breath. "Ma'am," she begins, "you can see my chart, right? You can see that I have taken the pills you want to prescribe me more than once. You can see that they haven't worked. Now my doctor told me that there is another possibility. Can't you see how frustrating it is to be told that I can only have access to a medication that I know won't work?" She pauses as her voice breaks.

I am three seconds from tossing off my covers and at least getting to the curtain to open it. I know every nurse and doctor can hear what's going on, but no one intervenes. My husband is going to be so angry when I tell him that I got up before I was supposed to, but I can't just let this woman be abandoned.

As I gingerly swing my legs over the edge of the bed, I hear the Black woman ask, "What would you do if you were in pain and doctors would only prescribe you a medication that you and your primary physician know won't work? Would you just fill the prescription and go home?"

At that moment, something clicks with the doctor. For

the first time, she doesn't respond immediately. She is quiet as she considers the question.

"Okay," she relents, "let me call your primary's emergency line and see if we can come up with a plan." The annoyance has drained from her voice. She is no longer treating this Black woman like a petulant toddler, combative for no reason. I can hear in her voice that she is finally listening to the logic and the pain of her patient.

I lean back against the pillows and take a deep breath. All I've done is listened, and I am emotionally drained by the treatment this Black woman endured. I am fine, but I am desperate to go home where I, too, am believed.

The Aftermath

I AM SENT home the next day but told to stay in bed for twenty-four hours. I am obedient. A week later, it's time for my doctor's appointment to hear the results of the biopsy.

My nephologist tells me that my kidneys are suffering from two problems. The first is a hereditary condition, a rare genetic disorder. She explains it's typically benign, sometimes not impacting normal kidney function at all. However, this is clearly not the case for me. More surprisingly, the biopsy, coupled with the scans, reveals that my kidneys are 30 percent scar tissue. The combination of these two realities means that my kidney function is compromised enough that I will sometimes pee blood.

My doctor asks me again about injuries, but I have not had any recent revelations regarding my lower back. She then inquires about my use of over-the-counter medication, wondering aloud if my use of pain meds during my periods has contributed to the problem. She asks about sickness and infections. But after all the questions, we don't know for sure what caused the scarring. We just know the damage is done.

By the end of the appointment I am diagnosed with stage three chronic kidney disease. The vast majority of people who are diagnosed with chronic kidney disease are over age sixty. I am thirty-eight.

With this diagnosis comes a list of lifestyle changes, I have to make so that it doesn't become stage four or five— which could mean dialysis.

I must take a daily medication.

I must cut back on meat.

I must avoid caffeine.

I must exercise three to four times a week, but those exercises must be low impact.

I must drink two liters of water every day.

I must not pick up anything heavy. My six-year-old qualifies as heavy.

I must not do anything that will stress out my kidneys.

The list is making me dizzy. I try to write it all down, but I can barely see my own handwriting through the tears filling my eyes. I feel silly that I am trying not to cry. She didn't tell me my illness is terminal. It's not at the stage where I need dialysis or a transplant. Am I being overdramatic?

When I get home and repeat the list to my husband, I cry because I love cheeseburgers, and I don't want to cut back on cheeseburgers. Then I feel silly for getting emotional about cheeseburgers. It's not about the cheeseburgers. It's the acceptance of this new reality. It's getting used to being someone who has a chronic condition. It is the realization that I will have to do many things—including how I hold my son—differently.

Once upon a time, all my body's organs were simply

drawings on a page in health class that I had to label in exchange for a gold star. But between pregnancy, labor, and now CKD, I know my body's internal life is real.

While I hate to get all "woo-woo," I am convinced that the hereditary condition I already possessed was made worse by being a Black woman in America. By the time I'm sitting in the doctor's office, I've been doing racial justice work for more than a decade. I've tried to help make sense of a world that would kill Trayvon Martin and Tamir Rice, that would explain the uprisings in Ferguson and Baltimore, that would offer context for a white supremacist walking into a Black church and opening fire. I've stood before coworkers and strangers, speaking truth to power and in return being insulted and screamed at. I've survived more microaggressions and macroaggressions than I have time to name. America has broken my heart over and over again with the double standard, the hypocrisy, the malignancy that is antiblackness. I have had to defend myself, defend my community, defend my people.

I didn't have words for my hypothesis until I read a book called *Weathering: The Extraordinary Stress of Ordinary Life in an Unjust Society* by Arlene Geronimus. In it she expounds on the relationship between a racially unjust society and its impact on people of color—particularly Black people. Using stories, case studies, and statistics, Professor Geronimus makes clear that systemic racism adversely affects our physical wellness. It weathers us, wearing on our bodies. Her book was helpful for exploring what my intuition was already telling me—that navigating uninterrogated whiteness is bad for our health.

I didn't yet have that language, but because I exist in a Black woman's body, I knew there was only one place to go with my suspicions that my work had contributed to my illness: other Black women. Black women would believe me. The first person I reached out to was Tarana Burke, activist, writer, and founder of MeToo. She had recently released a book in which she was open about her own health journey. So even though Tarana and I had never met in person, having only collaborated on one project together, I believed with my whole heart she would understand me. I sent her a message.

"Tarana," I wrote, "I have just been diagnosed with chronic kidney disease, and I feel certain this illness is connected to my work. I feel awful for saying this, but I think I have to do this work differently. I think it could kill me. I am committed to the Struggle—I don't mind living for it, but I don't want to die for it. I honor those who did, but I don't want to be a martyr. I want to live." And then I pushed send.

Once I did, I just stared at my phone, unsure about what to do with myself. My decision to reach out had been a little impulsive. I didn't even double-check that message for typos. I try not to pile work on Black women—I know that women like Tarana are constantly being asked to attend to others. I never want to be a burden to them, draining their energy. For a moment I considered deleting the message, but before I could she had written back.

She understood exactly what I was saying.

I sat down on my bed to read her words. I was nervous. I felt so vulnerable, both making confession of my chronic illness and breaking the first commandment of racial justice work: to give it everything. I leaned back against my pillows, took a deep breath, and started reading. Her response was a balm to my soul.

I won't share all the specifics, but I will say that in the first paragraph she told me more about her own health journey. In the second paragraph she told me that I wasn't alone. In the third paragraph she shared a few examples of other Black women in her life who are also suffering from chronic conditions that no one associates with Black women.

By this time tears were running down my face. I had been beating myself up for "allowing" this to happen. But it wasn't just me. I am not the only young Black woman suffering from a chronic disease. As I read about her list of girlfriends, I thought about my own. The one with COPD. The ones with autoimmune diseases. The ones who can't kick their infections. The ones with MS. The ones with migraines. The ones who have been going to doctors for years trying to get a diagnosis for the pain in their bodies. I am not alone.

In her final paragraph, Tarana gave me permission.

"Finding joy, finding what's on the other side of resiliency is also Movement work," she wrote. "Save your life."

Tarana gives me permission. Permission to pursue joy. Permission to rethink my work. Permission to abide by my own truth. Permission to pursue what I want for my self.

Thank you, Tarana.

Tests

AFTER MY DIAGNOSIS comes a slew of checkups and check-ins. With every doctor's visit, I first have to complete lab work, which means getting poked with a needle and peeing in a cup. The only thing that changes from visit to visit is how many vials of blood the vampires will need this time. (In my house we love all things horror, so it's fun to think I am required to visit the vampire's lair for my own health.)

Anyway, I was getting tested so often that at one point, the receptionist warned me, "I see you and your doctor are trying to stay on top of your numbers, but you should know if you continue at this rate, you will get a call from your insurance carrier that they won't cover these tests anymore." It was a lot to process.

It was a lot of walking into waiting rooms worried about what health conditions would be discovered this time. It was a lot of blood pressure cuffs while I worried about what my numbers would reveal. It was a lot of needles and a lot of vials of blood while I turned my head so I didn't have to watch the bottles fill. I became an expert at peeing in the cup but worried about what my kidneys hadn't filtered out. And after a year and a half of trying to keep up, I stopped. I stopped getting lab work done. I stopped making appointments. I stopped getting physicals. I just stopped.

To be clear, I do not recommend this as a health strategy. All of us should continue to welcome our doctors' assistance. But I want to tell the truth about my own journey. I hit a wall. I couldn't do it anymore. I was consumed by worry, and I just needed the worrying to stop.

During that time, I realized I wasn't overwhelmed by the actual lab work; though not pleasant, it was relatively easy. I could show up—no appointment necessary. It always took less than half an hour. The vampires were kind and good at their jobs. What overwhelmed me were the results of that lab work.

The MyChart notification "Your test results are in" would send me tumbling down a rabbit hole. Were these numbers good or bad? Better or worse? High or low? What does Google have to say about these seven words that I cannot pronounce? Where is the line graph that tells me if I'm trending up or down or stable, and what do we want that line to be doing?

The same thing happened in the doctor's office. No matter how kind or patient or matter-of-fact the doctor was toward me, my heart would beat loudly in my ears as I desperately tried to listen to what my results meant. I had to remind myself to breathe. I sat in every appointment waiting to be told that I was failing, and that my failing was going to make me increasingly sick.

I could handle the needles. I could handle the blood. I

could handle the cup. It was clarifying to discern that everything after the tests was what I feared.

Each time I prepared for an appointment, I braced myself for judgment. Did I exercise often enough? Was I eating well enough? Did I allow myself to get too stressed? Did I do more damage? Did I pass or did I fail? Every few weeks, I felt like I was sitting in front of a mean teacher who would never say "Well done" or "Look at your progress" or "I'm so proud of you." Just a pass. Or a fail.

The results never felt like a checkup of how my body was doing. They felt like a judgment of *me*.

So I avoided the testing to avoid the self-judgment. The only way I could silence my inner critic was to starve it of anything it could assess. I still did my best with regard to my list of do's and don'ts. But I just couldn't go through the pass-fail judgment anymore . . . for a little while.

Of course, I knew I couldn't avoid lab work forever. This was still a relatively new diagnosis for me, and as my doctors prescribed medications and changes to my lifestyle, it was important that we all knew how my body was responding. I couldn't ignore a chronic condition, so I had to learn how to face the self-judgment.

I sat down and looked at the test results already in MyChart. I sat with the feeling of opening the website, of staring at the numbers, of not knowing what half of the words meant. I opened the line charts, which showed the changes in my numbers over time. As I sat with all the data points taken over the previous year of my life, it occurred to me that each tiny circle was just one day. "It's only a snapshot," I said to myself. Each data point could only reveal how I was doing at that moment—not how I'd be doing forever. All those tests and numbers and words explained how my body was reacting to a number of different stimulants, including medicine, water intake, workouts, emotional stress, and more. Even the time of day could cast a different picture. My lab work was less a test and more an assessment of how my body was doing right at that moment. It was a freeing realization.

The next time I went in for lab work, I repeated the sentence to myself over and over again: "It's just a snapshot of today." As I peed into the cup, "It's just a snapshot of today." As my blood filled the vials, "It's just a snapshot of today." When the results showed up on my phone, "It's just a snapshot of the day." Thinking about the results as snapshots of my body, as opposed to verdicts on my own commitment to myself was extraordinarily helpful in taming the worry.

Perhaps the numbers revealed I was under more stress. Or perhaps they revealed a medication that wasn't quite right. Or perhaps they revealed my kidneys' appreciation for my giant Stanley cup because I was actually drinking two liters of water a day. Rather than beat myself up for not exerting control, I sought to understand what my body wanted to tell me through this snapshot.

I have decided to stop judging my body and myself for how it navigates a racist, imperialist, capitalist, patriarchal society that disrespects Black women with impunity. My body is doing its best to survive in a world that was not created with my thriving in mind. And my body is doing its absolute best to keep going. When I get these tests done, my doctor is just saying, "Okay, your kidneys are a little more stressed than usual right now." And since I cannot fix the world, what I can do is be gentler with my kidneys by increasing this dose of medication. Or maybe I can be more kind to my kidneys over the next month by making sure I get most of my protein from peanut butter or egg whites, instead of cheeseburgers.

Reframing the tests as not being about my character or commitment gave me an opportunity to listen to my body and try new ways of caring for it, to see if they make a difference. Sometimes it does. Sometimes it doesn't. But my commitment to myself, to loving myself in a world that often doesn't, is my nonnegotiable.

Now, if I can just get myself to make a dentist appointment . . .

I Love Myself When
I Am Sad

It was a fine cry—loud and long—but it had no bottom and it had no top, just circles and circles of sorrow.

—TONI MORRISON,
Sula

The Screening

IT'S 2:58 A.M. and the baby is crying.

It's 2:59 A.M. and the baby is crying.

It's 3:00 A.M. and the baby is crying.

It's 3:01 A.M. and the baby is crying.

I am watching the second hand move its way around the clock. I can't hear the tiny click when the minute hand finally moves, but I know it's there. The shadows cast by the streetlights into our apartment are elongated across the white walls. Everything is completely still except the tiny human in my arms.

I am bouncing and patting and shushing, but also I cannot take my eyes off the clock.

3:02 A.M.

3:03 A.M.

3:04 A.M.

I'm beginning to spiral. My inability to quiet my child is going to wake up my husband, and the dog, and the neighbors. His crying sounds louder and louder to me.

I tear my eyes away from the clock and peer down at him. I plod from the open space of the living room to his bedroom and shut the door behind me. Every cry rips through my brain. I cannot think straight. I walk over to his closet. And then I get in it. I feel myself sliding down the wall, to the floor. I am helpless.

I cannot make the baby stop crying. I cannot control the bleeding from my vagina. I cannot poop without wanting to pass out. I cannot stop my milk from leaking or my nipples from hurting. I am in control of nothing. And responsible for everything. And I have to get help.

What I get when I go in for my six-week checkup is a quiz.

And a rating system asking me to pick a number, one through five.

This is a portion of the quiz:

I have been able to laugh and see the funny side of things.

Well, I'm Black. Seeing the funny side of things is basically my whole existence, or else I and everyone in my community would succumb to absolute rage and burn this country to the ground. Then you wouldn't be giving me this test.

I have looked forward with enjoyment to things.

To things? Like the possibility of sleeping one day? Yes, I look forward to that. I can finally eat deli meat again, so I can't wait to have a turkey bacon club sandwich. Does that count?

I have blamed myself unnecessarily when things went wrong.

"Unnecessarily." What does that mean? I put the bottles in the dishwasher but forget to actually run it. I've been pumping, but I didn't label a batch and now I can't figure out if that milk is usable or not. Things are going wrong. And I'm pretty sure it's my fault.

I have been anxious or worried for no good reason.

Seriously? No good reason? I am a first-time parent. I am worried about EVERYTHING. I have been eating cereal for dinner a couple times a week for most of my adulthood, and now I have to actually maintain the nutritional needs of a baby human. I am worried all the time.

I have felt scared and panicky for no good reason.

Sigh. No good reason again? People, I went to one parenting class, and you all scared the shit out of me over laying the baby down on his stomach or accidentally falling asleep with him in my bed. Is there a list on the back of this sheet that tells me which are the good reasons to be "scared and panicky" and which are the bad reasons?

Things have been getting to me.

Things like my parents being upset that I don't warm the bottles? Things like trying to figure out how to breast-feed without my toes curling in pain every time this child grazes my nipples? Things like juggling work and taking care of this baby at the same time? Things like organizing schedules and creating routines and attempting to hold on to a single thought that disappears as soon as I leave one room and enter the next? Nope. None of these are getting to me. Not at all.

I have been so unhappy that I have had difficulty sleeping.

I am having difficulty sleeping because my baby is uninterested in sleeping. If my child was sleeping and I wasn't, maybe then I could ascertain the nature of my insomnia.

I have felt sad or miserable.

Yes. My whole life has just turned upside down, and I am not sure what I'm doing. I have felt sadness. What I don't know is whether the amount of sadness I'm feeling is normal or not. Can we pour my sadness into a measuring cup so that you can weigh it and tell me if I am above or below an average amount of sadness?

I have been so unhappy that I have been crying.

I cried the first time I pooped. And the second time. And the third time. I am crying more than I would usually cry. I don't usually cry when I poop, but here I am. Everything is different, and tears are involved. I am happy to have this child. But I also cry a lot. I do not know how to resolve these two things when I read this question.

The thought of harming myself has occurred to me.

This feels like the first clear question I have read on this test. No, I have not been thinking about harming myself.

Maybe if they had added one more question—does this test make you angry?—I would have known right then that I was definitely depressed.

. . .

THE TEST WAS not helpful for me. I now know that standing in my son's closet sliding down the wall should have been a clue that I was depressed. And yet, I can tell you it seemed like a completely reasonable response in the moment. Here were the aha moments when I finally figured out something wasn't right:

1. When I reach for the last tissue in the tissue box, it occurs to me that I have sobbed more in the last month than I'd done the whole prior year. I am that girl who cries at a good commercial. However, full-on sobbing is typically an every-other-year experience for me. I'm generally too good at numbing for weeping. Yet now I have cleaned out a whole tissue box on my own in a month. That sticks out as unusual for me.

2.   One night at 3:00 A.M., when I am listless during another feeding session, I wonder what it might be like to leave. I don't form an actual plan. I don't grab my keys or decide where I will go. I don't even put the baby down. I have no desire to hurt myself or my sweet boy. In fact, I don't want to cause anyone harm. I just wonder for a moment what it might be like to slip away to a vague somewhere else. And it feels incongruous with how much I deeply love my son, my growing family, my home. The incongruity is what makes me think something must be wrong. My brain feels completely disconnected from my heart.

3.   My dad gifted my husband and me a weekend away. (We spent two nights at a nearby hotel, where we fell asleep holding hands. It was so erotic.) But when we stepped onto the elevator to head to our room, Tommie asked, "Do you miss him yet?" And I chuckled and replied, "Not yet. We've only been gone for twenty minutes." Then I looked at him quizzically and asked, "Do *you* miss him already?" Tommie's response was an easy "Of course."

Well shit.

That's when it dawned on me that motherhood was only worry for me. That's what the questions were trying to ask. I had been assessing whether or not I had *good* reasons for my worry, for my fear, for my panic. But in that moment, standing in a hotel, with my baby safely in the care of the man who raised me, I was free of trepidation for the first time since my little guy entered the world. It wasn't that I didn't miss my son. I just didn't miss the total anxiety that had consumed me.

Even after I admitted to myself that I was falling apart at the seams, my first inclination was not to get help. It was to blame myself. I kept whispering, "Get it together, Austin." I chided myself for not practicing enough self-care. I wasn't getting outside enough. I wasn't showering often enough. I wasn't exercising while pushing Baby in his stroller. I was ordering too much takeout. I wasn't chatting with my friends. Every day I felt crushed under the weight of all the ways I was failing.

I have long rejected the idea of being a "strong Black woman," but that phrase is more than just an identity descriptor. Many of us made a point of hanging up our capes a long time ago, but the truth is we have had to be strong. It's how we made it this far. It has been less of a goal to reach than our collective reality.

We have been expected to save the world from itself over and over again. We have been expected to be the driving force of every progressive social movement and ask for nothing in return. We have been expected to rightly divide humanity and monsters and still raise our families, raise our communities. We must advocate for ourselves at school and then at work and in places of worship and the communities where we volunteer and organize. It's not a conscious decision. It is the way we have been expected to move through the world.

Now I was being a strong Black woman, again, by trying to power through my panic and fear and worry and sadness. I didn't set out to be a strong Black woman, and yet strength is what I demanded from myself. I was conditioned for it.

And then my college roommate, Jessica, who also happens to be a doula, sent me a text the day before my next doctor's visit.

You ok?

> I'm honestly not sure.

What do you mean?

> I'm not sure if what I feel is normal or
> not normal? Everything I feel seems
> so rational. But I just don't know.

Maybe you can talk to your doctor?

> I've tried. I've tried explaining why I
> feel how I feel and asking "aren't
> those good reasons to feel what I
> feel?" But all they keep saying is
> "that sounds stressful."

Anxiety is real. Sleeplessness is real.
Keeping your new baby alive and
well is real. But also the hormone shifts
and dumps and healing you are going
through are real. There is zero shame
in needing meds or any/all support.

Everything has been so hard to navigate, let alone name.

Listen. If you could will your way out of this,
you would. I would too. But hormones and
neurotransmitters don't seem to give a crap
about what we wish. And I've done all the
things. Vitamins. Yoga. Tea. Herbs. And all
that is good. But it doesn't replace meds.

That final message set me free. This wasn't about my willpower. This wasn't about my own failure to get it together or grow up or calm down. This wasn't about me needing to *do* better—to be more consistent with naps and vitamins and baths and quiet time and long walks and exercise. Those were all things rooted in my willpower, in the idea of being stronger.

My body had changed dramatically, and my brain was not immune from that change. I needed a pump for my milk. I needed ice packs for my vag. I needed Motrin for my uterus. And my brain needed something, too: medication.

At my next appointment, when my doctor says, "How are you doing?" I tell her the truth: "I think I might be depressed." Instead of going through the quiz, I simply share what feels true to me. I *feel* like I can't pull it together. I *feel* like I haven't slept in ages. I *feel* worn out. I *feel* overwhelmed. I end every day *feeling* like a failure. Without judging any of these statements, I simply share how I am experiencing the world right now. And she agrees. I need help.

She prescribes an antidepressant and explains that it could take up to six weeks before I feel the effects. But within three days, I felt the difference. I remember stepping out of my apartment to walk to my car. When I hit the sidewalk, the warmth of the beaming sun held me in place for a second. I looked at the sky and said aloud, "God, the sun feels so good." I stood there for a few moments longer with my eyes closed. I'm sure I looked ridiculous. It was late summer and the weather was regularly warm. But I hadn't had a thought like that in weeks . . . in months . . . in almost a year.

I knew right then that I didn't just have postpartum blues. I'd been experiencing depression at least since the early stages of pregnancy. I could notice the sun, but I could not feel it. I had forgotten the difference between noticing and feeling. I could notice joy, but I could not sense it in my body. It wasn't until the *feeling* returned that I became conscious of how long I had gone without it.

Now I could go outside and take walks because I could

feel the sun. I could wake up in the middle of the night and feed my baby because I could hear him sucking down the milk and feel myself laugh at the bigness of the burps escaping his tiny body. I enjoyed eating because I could taste my food again. My joy was enough to move me through sleeplessness and stress and uncertainty. I panicked less when joy was present in my body as an experience, and not just in my mind as a vague knowing. For the first time, I didn't have to lean into strength to power me through motherhood. I could lean into joy. I could stop being a strong Black woman when I became a joyful one.

I want more joy for Black women. I imagine it would make us more powerful in ways that serve us . . . and I don't really care what it does or doesn't do for the world. We deserve the world for once.

Hate

I AM NO stranger to hateful messages. They are tweeted, instagrammed, and facebooked in my direction. I receive emails and direct messages that would make your skin crawl. Some are filled with nothing but the n-word. Others the b-word. Most are concoctions of sexism and racism that only women of color ever receive. Most are misspelled.

But this is different.

Snail mail doesn't come directly to my apartment. Instead I have to cross campus to the mailroom in the residence life department offices. I mostly collect letters regarding my student loans. But today there is a bulky envelope amidst all the slim ones. It catches my eye because my name is scrawled in thin black handwriting.

I grab it along with the other random envelopes and stop to chat with the women who keep our office running. After walking back across campus, I unlock my door and drop all the envelopes on a small side table. The one with my hand-printed name catches my eye again.

I know my father's handwriting, and this is not it. I know my mother's handwriting, and this is not it. I know my grandmother's handwriting, and this is not it. I eye the spot where a return label should be and find nothing.

When I open it, I discover two typed pages of hate mail.

The letter doesn't call me four-letter words. It doesn't include a death threat. In fact, it reads almost polite. Or at least as polite as a stranger can be in discounting my life experience. For two pages, the author hands me his manifesto. He informs me that I am incorrect about my understanding of the world, of America. For two pages the author demands that I write with more grace and patience for white people. For two pages the author criticizes me, declaring that I don't truly have a grasp on being Black in America, and if I just knew the Black people that he knows, I would have a greater understanding of everything. For two pages the author describes why he is superior to me, listing his degrees, his church posts, his standing in his community. For two pages this author insults my intelligence and my work. He insists that I am wrong.

It is not so much the content that I find disconcerting, offensive though it is. What makes this different is that I am holding it in my hands. This is different because someone typed a letter. Printed the letter. Stuffed the letter into an envelope. Bought a stamp. Found my address and went to a post office or mailbox to send it to me. That's so much work, just to tell me you don't like what I stand for, and that you know how to find me. I am struck by the amount of work. I find that kind of work ethic behind contempt to be frightening. Especially since I live where I work.

My nervous system is flooded with questions. *Does this person know I work where I live, or does he think he sent this note only to my job? Does this person visit campus? Is he regularly on campus? Have I passed by him before? Will I tomorrow? If I don't change my opinions or write less forcibly on the internet, what will he do next? Will he keep sending notes? Will this escalate? Am I unsafe?*

And now this is my day. This is my day because I don't feel safe. Whatever I had planned for myself—meetings, social gatherings, napping, eating, writing, teaching—is on hold. My day is now figuring out what steps I need to take to restore a sense of safety, or at the very least leave clues should something happen to me.

My day is now duplicating the letter so that I can leave copies with my supervisors. My day is now walking over to our campus security to confer with them about the level of danger I am in. My day is now talking to my husband about our personal security measures and how we keep me safe on a largely open campus. My day is now deciding how much I want to investigate this letter—do I look up the company on the letterhead (yes, it was on company letterhead). Do I look into the list of accolades and see if it helps me pinpoint who this is? Should I read it a second time, third time, fourth time to search for clues about him and his intentions? On some level I am used to receiving hate mail. It never feels good, or even neutral, honestly. What I find more vexing, though, is the time, energy, thought that I must expend in response to the hate.

The dreams I dream for Black women to do other things with our time than document the hate used to intimidate us . . . just in case.

Home

IT'S NOT UNUSUAL for Black homeownership to result from the tragic or the miraculous. Because our parents, grandparents, and great-grandparents were largely locked out of homeownership opportunities, many of us can't acquire the cash for a down payment until someone in our family passes away. Occasionally someone we know will "make it big" after prevailing through systems not always intended for our own success—like the entertainment or sports industry. But barring that kind of miracle, many Black folks are still waiting for the wealth benefits of ownership to accrue in the way they've done for white families.

And so, as for many people who are Gen X or millennials, the prospect of my husband and me ever buying a house was a long shot. Our rent was more than enough to cover a mortgage, but we'd never had the cash for a down payment. That is, until my book, *I'm Still Here,* did the impossible and reached *The New York Times* bestsellers list in 2020. What also happened in 2020? A Black man, George Floyd, was murdered, and books on race in America, including mine, were trending everywhere. With one royalty check, we suddenly had enough cash to start a home search—our own miracle, but inseparable from a tragedy.

Driving from showing to showing, we meander through the neighborhood first to gain some insight about our possible neighbors. We take note when there are a lot of Blue Lives Matter signs in the yards. We skip the house with a six-foot Trump 2020 sign directly across the street. We don't need to enter the one with a tiny confederate flag in the living room window. At every house, we ask ourselves, *Will our little boy be able to ride his bike safely here? Will he be able to knock on the neighbor's door if he is lost or has an emergency? Will my husband be mistaken for a criminal while he is walking the dog? Will I be assumed to be a trespasser while I take a morning stroll?* We scan the streets looking for literal signs of safety.

And then we find it: the house we love. Pulling up to our home is a joyous event every single day. For a couple who had a hard time imagining we would ever have the cash, credit, and credibility necessary to buy a home, it still feels like a wonder to pull into our driveway. Our neighborhood is diverse, and we are often met with smiles and small talk from our neighbors—all except one.

Despite our best efforts, we discovered that we have a Karen living next door.

One summer we had to completely tear up our backyard to fix a water issue with our foundation. The crew, made up of Black men, was hard at work when one of them called my husband.

"Hey, man," he says, "we are going to stop work for a little bit. We left our paperwork at the office and think we should go get it."

"Why?" my husband asks, concerned. "We have the permits, and our documents are all displayed. Why do you feel like you need additional paperwork on you?"

"Because your neighbor is watching us and she has her camera out," he replies nervously.

"What?" my husband asks, confused.

"She's taping us," he says.

"Taping you?" Tommie repeats incredulously. He takes a deep breath, now understanding why the guys would be so uncomfortable.

"Listen, I own this home. We have all of our permits and permissions. You are not doing anything wrong. I'm here, and I promise you can continue to work. She is trippin' but I am here."

Tommie tells them to keep their phones nearby and to call or text if the woman approaches them.

The guys feel better and continue to work. We peek out our windows every so often to make sure Karen doesn't cross into our yard or speak to them.

A couple hours later, our doorbell rings. It's her. She hasn't spoken to us in the two years we've lived next door, but today she is on our doorstep. "Hi, I just saw this package here and wanted to give it to you."

My husband is blinking in shock. He turns to me to announce who is at the door: "Our neighbor wanted to bring us the package *on our porch*," he calls out.

They talk for a few moments more, then Tommie closes the door and walks into the kitchen, where I'm making dinner. "Apparently, she is concerned about the landscaping vehicles breaking the heads on her underground sprinklers as the crew moves between our houses."

"Okay," I respond, waiting for the rest, knowing there is more.

"She has some flags she wants to put in the ground to mark her sprinkler system."

"Ahhhh, so when she sent the photos to our housing association, she discovered they already knew and wouldn't be stopping our crew?"

"Basically," he replies.

"All right, time to tag-team. If one of us is going to make the white woman cry, it has to be me. You stay here. I'll meet her out front."

I talk to myself as I walk to her yard. I understand the desire to protect her sprinkler system—she uses it regularly, and we cannot see where each spout is located. I'm not here for her intimidation of the crew, but I'll use her flags if she'll leave us alone.

"Hi," I say when I've reached the line where our yards meet. "My husband says you're worried about your sprinklers."

"Oh yes," she says. "I've had them break before, and it's so expensive to fix. I mean I don't know if perhaps some of them are already broken—" she suggests breathlessly.

Before she starts to spiral, I interrupt.

"Well, we wouldn't want them broken, either. Why don't

you hand me those flags, and you go turn on your system. I'll plant a flag at each sprinkler head so the guys can make sure to never hit them, even by accident. And we'll be able to see that they are all still in working order right now."

She is a little jumpy but hands me the flags and scurries into her garage to turn on the water system. I plant the little flags while she makes her way back over to me. "Everything look good?" I ask like I'm placating a child. That's how I feel.

"Oh yes," she says and launches into another explanation for why this is important to her.

I cut her off again. "Well, I'm glad you let us know, because this was an easy solution. All right?"

I turn to leave, but now that she's no longer worried about damages, her curiosity has taken over. "So you all have a lot of work going on back there . . ."

"Yes, we do," I tell her. "Just getting some waterproofing done."

"Oh, we had to do that, too. Thankfully we haven't had a problem since," she shares.

"That's good to know," I say shortly, still trying to smoothly end this conversation.

"You know I thought you all might be putting in a pool."

It takes everything in me to fix my face. I know she has taken pictures and/or video, which means she can clearly see my foundation exposed across the length of my house. Why would I put a pool at my foundation?

"No, at least not right now," I respond, "just trying to protect our foundation."

"Wait." She responds. "You aren't renting?" she asks next.

Now she is really testing my patience. So because we are a Black couple, we must be renting? Why would anyone install an inground pool at a house they're renting? The leaps of logic white people have to make to prop up their own racism are staggering.

My face clearly wasn't fixed enough, because she rushes on. "You know, there are just so many people renting in this neighborhood now."

I purposefully don't answer, looking from house to house, knowing that all of them are homeowners. I turn back to her, looking her in the eyes. "No. This house. Is mine."

I have put on my unbothered voice for too long now. The battery life on my patience is draining, and I'm afraid that anything I say next will result in tears—hers, not mine. I would very much like to return to the silence that existed between us before today.

"Okay, well, I have to head back inside," I conclude. "Thanks again for letting us know of your concerns. Have a good evening."

I walk away without looking back.

Once inside, I relay the conversation to Tommie. We both agree that when our child is old enough to play outside on his own, he needs to stay to the right of our house to avoid Karen. We want to do our best to ensure our miracle doesn't become a tragedy.

I love my home. And I know that regardless of my zip code, I live in America, where too many people still believe I do not belong. Nonetheless, I will create my home anyway.

Gran

HER DARK SKIN looks papery but feels firm under my touch. I can see the veins running the length of her forearms. I am surprised by her strength when I lean into her. She is propping me up. With my face next to hers, I can hear the slight buzz of her right hearing aid. It almost looks like an Apple AirPod.

My grandmother currently lives on the Gulf Coast of Mississippi. She is visiting us in Metro Detroit for an extended family gathering. I've brought her upstairs, and we are laying down on the memory foam mattress of my pull-out. She's testing its comfort because I am desperate for her to stay with me instead of in a hotel. She has already decided it's comfortable enough to stay, but neither of us has gotten up.

Her silver hair perfectly frames her face, with a little help from expertly placed bobby pins. Her left hand dances in front of me as she talks. I know where all six gold rings and the Egyptian gold bracelet sliding down her wrist came from. It's been a long time since I've lain like this with her.

I have a flashback of being seven or eight. We are in her home in Cleveland. It's almost my bedtime, and we are both in our pajamas with our hair tied up in bonnets. My grandfather fills the doorframe on his way to the bathroom. He is six foot four; even bent over his cane, he still stands tall. I am being silly, putting on my grandmother's glasses, which were on the nightstand next to me. He gives his big laugh and asks, "Now which one of you is Gran?"

I am absolutely tickled by his question. I cannot stop laughing, and my laughter makes my grandmother laugh.

She is remembering him, too, in this moment. But not only him.

She talks about Midge, at least how Midge used to be. Midge has been her best friend since college, but now she "doesn't remember much of anything," my grandmother says with sadness.

"So many of my friends are gone," she states as a matter of fact. "Everyone just keeps dying." Gran is ninety-three, and while her age has allowed her to meet her great-grandchildren, that blessing has come with a cost.

She tells me about losing Iona Hancock. My gran and I loved visiting Iona. She was a firecracker, but after years of smoking, her lungs couldn't keep up any longer. "I was so mad at her," Gran recounts. "I went to visit her once and she was on oxygen still smoking!" Her indignation is still present. "I couldn't believe it," she says before falling silent. She takes a couple breaths, calming down. "But we did make up before she passed. I'm glad we made up."

She continues her list. There's PJ, the only man she

wanted to marry a decade after my grandfather died. My great-grandmother, who she cared for in the final years of her life. So many loved ones, gone.

So much loss.

"I'm just creating reasons to keep on going," she says. Gran has traveled the world. I ask if there is someplace left on her list to visit. "I'm thinking about taking a trip to Alaska. I've never really wanted to go to Alaska because it's cold, but I hear it might not be that cold because of global warming. Anyway, I need things to look forward to."

She gazes up at the ceiling, still holding me, rubbing my shoulder as she speaks.

"I just hope that when it's my time, it will be in my sleep."

The weight of her words settles around me. I worry I will crack under them, but I want her to keep telling me about her hope. Even if it hurts.

"Yes, I want it to be in my sleep. To fall asleep and just not wake up. That sounds peaceful. I hope it will be peaceful."

Usually when my grandmother starts talking about her mortality, I shush her. I tell her how much I still need her. I tell her how much she is loved by her children, her grandchildren, her great-grandchildren. I assure her of how very much she will be missed the moment she is gone.

But not this time.

This time we are not on the phone or chatting through FaceTime. This time I can hear her heartbeat, feel the rising of her chest with each inhale. This time I can sense the consideration, the deep wanting in her voice. This time I want her to know that I hear her.

I have so many hopes right now. Hopes for my career. Hopes for my child. Hopes for my marriage. Hopes for my friendships. My grandmother has experienced every one of those hopes.

But her hope isn't done yet. She has lived a full life, as she likes to say. But today she wants me to hear about her one remaining hope for her own future. Her hope for how she will die.

I roll over, placing my cheek on her shoulder and wrapping my arm around her tiny waist.

"I hope so, too, Gran," I whisper.

I haven't lost her yet. But I'm already sad for the day I will. The day her hope will come to pass.

I Love Myself When I Am Healing

What looks like crazy on an ordinary day looks a lot like love when you catch it in the moonlight.

—PEARL CLEAGE,
*What Looks Like Crazy
on an Ordinary Day*

Legacy

LIKE MANY BLACK folks, every year my dad's side of the family has a huge reunion. But in 2023, instead of going to the big one, my dad and his siblings decide to create a smaller one. We have been meeting regularly on Zoom throughout the pandemic and miss one another terribly. It's finally safe to meet in person again, and we want as much time together as possible. So we opt for the intimacy of being in Akron, Ohio, where all of my dad's siblings still live.

On the first night, my auntie brings a special guest. His name is Baby Dhay. He's the grandson of my cousin Dalin, who died in prison while I was in graduate school. We were gathered just like this when we learned that he was gone.

Baby Dhay is three years old, but already he is bursting with a personality so similar to the grandfather he never met, it hurts. It would be eerie if it wasn't also soothing. I can't take my eyes off of his huge brown ones. They seem to take up half his face, stopping only to make space for his still chunky cheeks.

He is tiny, but he walks like a grown man, taking sure-footed steps like he has important places to be. His head is high, and he has not an ounce of shyness as he moves between groups of us around and around the two-bedroom hotel suite.

At one point he climbs into the arms of his great-aunt Dionne and begs for a kiss. "No!" she playfully screams. "I don't want no kiss."

Undeterred, he holds her face in his tiny hands, determined to keep her still, despite her protests. "Let me give you kiss!" he says over and over, giggling as his great-aunt wiggles out of his grip.

Finally, she relents. "Okay, just ooooone kiss."

His eyes light up as he pokes out his little lips.

"Mmmm-mwhaaa," they both say together.

And I am undone.

No one needs me to get all sappy amidst the happy sounds of chatter and laughter, yet I find myself holding back tears. I am equal parts sadness and gratitude; the feeling is overwhelming. A little over ten years ago, I watched helplessly as Dionne fell into her mother's arms, learning that Dalin was gone. I will remember every moment of that day for the rest of my life. So will his mother. And his sister. And his girlfriend. And his daughter. But we aren't the only ones with a traumatic story rooted in the criminal justice system. In fact, we are far from alone.

Books, documentaries, studies, journal articles, and music have been created to illuminate incarceration rates, and the violence our criminal justice system wreaks on a disproportionately Black, male population. But what I cannot stop thinking about is the comparative lack of data for the emotional undoing of the Black women left behind. I wish it was possible to put the pain in equivalent terms.

I wonder how many oceans we could fill with the tears cried in hearings and funerals. I wonder how many hot-air balloons we could raise with the sighs we have breathed from our toes. I wonder how many miles we have traveled, how many songs we have sung, on the meandering roads between homes and prison facilities. I wonder how much paper, how much ink, how many picture frames have been charged with reminding us of loved ones lost to the system or snatched from this earth. I wonder how much strength is contained in the combined tightness of our muscles, the stress of holding everything together or avoiding the question *What did you do over the weekend?* Because "visited the prison or laid flowers at a grave site" isn't considered polite conversation in the workplace. I wonder how heavy the silence would be if we placed our unspoken words on a scale. I wonder how many of us are buried in the ground because we gave our all to fight against the system in honor of our loved ones. I wonder how many Black women have themselves been swept into the criminal justice system and have hardly told a soul.

The emotional lives of Black women are complex, and part of that complexity is grief. Because grief doesn't die, even when we must swallow it and pretend we are fine. I bet we could power every major city in America with the energy it takes to push down our sadness and convincingly proclaim that we are good.

But right now. In this moment. At this reunion. We are good. We made it through the storm, and now here is Dionne, showered in kisses from her little brother's grandson as he bounces on her lap.

Our grief is not gone, but neither is our joy. How devastatingly sweet to witness Dalin's legacy go on . . . and in such a beautiful, brown package.

Wealth

I GREW UP with white people who had generational wealth. Some had trust funds and new cars and payments for their first year of rent. Others could start businesses, fail, and start new ones with their parents' help. Most didn't have to pay for their own weddings and took honeymoons on the other side of the world. They had access to job opportunities and strong networks and their last names on buildings.

We don't have that. But we could have.

I come from Black folks who weren't just poor. They were made poor. They were locked out of America's opportunities for advancement. They were not given wages, and then they were not given equal wages. They were forced into a system of indebted farming, even after emancipation. Too often, they were deprived of homeownership and business permits. White folks banned them from an education, and so they created their own schoolhouses, colleges, and universities. In the instances when Black folks stole the keys and created opportunities for themselves anyway, that success was often followed by lynchings, white riots, the stealing of land, and even bombings. Our families were not poor. We were made poor.

And so we had to create a different kind of wealth.

In my family we hold close the wealth of our elders, the heirlooms they left for us. We have my grandmother's art-work, charcoal-etched figures that somehow resemble each of us, even though she drew them long before we were born. We have Bibles with cracked spines that have been passed down from generation to generation. We have my great-grandmother's fur coats and invitations to formal so-cial events held in the forties. We have my grandfather's briefcase, where he carefully placed all his papers for play-ing the numbers. And we have recipes. So many recipes.

We have pound cake recipes. We have fried chicken rec-ipes. We have deviled egg recipes. We have recipes on tidy index cards and recipes on the backs of envelopes. We have recipes cut out from magazines that we then made our own. We have recipes handwritten from memory on yellowed paper, stained from ingredients past.

The first time I tried making my grandmother's dinner rolls, I contacted my aunt for the recipe. She wrote it out for me and gave as many specific directions as she could. I mea-sured out the flour. I added the salt. I filled a little measuring cup with water. I ripped open the yeast packet, and . . . tears. Tears streamed down my face. The yeast packet smelled like her house at Christmas. It was a smell I had no idea I missed so much. A smell I equated with her and family and love and warmth and laughter. I stood in the middle of the kitchen, crying.

Those rolls turned out terribly. It was probably too much salt from my tears.

Every couple years I would try again, this time delighting in knowing the familiar fragrance would soon overtake my kitchen. But still, they never quite turned out right. It didn't bother me. I felt more like I was communing with her than trying to make a delicious meal.

Ten years later, on a Zoom call during the pandemic, I asked my aunt to send me the recipe again. It was buried under years of emails. I hadn't tried to make it in the midst of pregnancy and new motherhood. But my baby was five, and it felt like the kind of capricious ritual I could resume.

"Wait!" she shouts to everyone on the call. "What if we bake them together? That way I can teach you all the steps that don't make sense when written out."

We set a date. My parents and my little sister drive to my home. Two aunts, two cousins, and an uncle join in the fun from their homes scattered around Ohio. We are all in our kitchens, with bowls and measuring cups and ingredients everywhere.

Two hours later, we are all covered in dustings of flour, our hands still sticky from handling the dough. We bite into our rolls at the same time. And for a moment, our homes are connected by the same smell, the same food, the same story, the same taste, the same wealth.

We have a healing generational wealth. A wealth that keeps us rooted to our past and tethered to one another. We have generational wealth that meets us in our grief, that inspires joy, that we purposefully pass on. We are wealthy, too.

Assistance

THANKS TO FRIENDS and doctors, I now have help—lots
of help—in the form of maintenance meds. I love that term,
"maintenance meds." I'm not sure where I first heard it, but
it resonated deeply. I am a high-maintenance kind of girl,
but not in terms of my clothes, perfume, or makeup. I don't
own a lot of shoes or purses or jewelry, but I have a body
that requires some additional help to function in this world.

In order to make it through each day I need the help of
my partner, my family, my friends, and a team of meds. And
while I sometimes have to make changes to my roster, I will
likely have a team for the rest of life. They are a part of how
I maintain my body and my sanity.

I have Happy Pills. These are my antidepressants. They
don't actually make me happy in and of themselves—that's
a different kind of drug. But my happy pills allow me to feel
sensations that I otherwise could only report dispassion-
ately. They take me from "Yes, I can see the sun is shining"
to "Yes, the sun feels warm."

When I came home with my new prescription, the first
thing I did was contact my mom and dad. I put them on the
same text message, which I rarely do. I explained that I told

the doctor I was struggling and she offered an antidepressant. I wasn't sure what either of their reactions would be; it just felt important to me as a new mom to reach out to my own parents. They both immediately replied, "I'm so proud of you." My mom even revealed that she had struggled with depression when I was born. I cried again, partly because the meds were still brand new, but also because I didn't expect my mom and dad to be proud. I thought they might be accepting, but that's not what they said. They said they were proud. Proud that I was honest. Proud that I was getting the help that I needed. I want this freedom for all Black women—to be able to talk about the struggle of depression or anxiety or mental health needs and not only receive acceptance but know they have made their families proud.

I have Sunny Pills, too. It's not uncommon for Black people to have a vitamin D deficiency, and I am one of them. So my doctor has encouraged me to take a daily dose. She would love it if I would also take a daily Steel Pill (iron pills) but I have yet to find some that are both inexpensive and won't make me sick.

I have Period Pills, also known as a contraceptive. These little pills and their counterparts have many more uses beyond preventing pregnancy, but I take them so I can get my sexy on without the probability of conceiving.

I have Organ Pills. Now that I have definitive proof that those little drawings of humans with organs inside are in fact real, I have learned that some of my inside parts need help. They don't always function at their highest capacity. Some of them will never function that way again. So they need extra support.

To help me keep track of my teammates, I have a twenty-eight-day pill pack. I purchased the smallest I could find, but it's still the size of a purse. For the first few months, when I pulled it out of my drawer with my giant glass of water, I felt like a ninety-year-old woman. All the sensuality would drain out of my body. I no longer felt youthful. I no longer felt sexy. I no longer felt like myself. I felt broken. And I wondered if my husband felt like he was sleeping with Granny.

Sometimes I still struggle to keep this feeling at bay. Doctors' visits, gowns, therapy appointments, blood pressure cuffs, needles, pills, shots, IV bags, and all the other things we must endure to care for bodies experiencing chronic illness, often don't leave us feeling human—let alone desirable, even to ourselves.

But I am not broken, I've realized; I'm just high maintenance.

This is why the term "maintenance meds" is so helpful for me. My body simply requires more than it used to in order to get through each day. She's been through a lot. She has survived microaggressions and macroaggressions. She has survived pregnancy and labor and postlabor. She has survived falls and bruises and scars. She has been through a multitude of moves, emotional upheavals, and traumatic surprises. She has walked me through grief time and time again. She has felt unsafe and she has been unsafe. Every day, I ask her to walk through a patriarchal, white supremacist, capitalist world and defy it. I ask her to remain human, and in so doing, I have discovered that she is not a heartless machine, with parts that are easily replaced. I am human. And I require assistance to stay alive.

Glowing

BRENDA AND GAIL are my play Mom and Auntie. They have been watching over me for a long time. I met Brenda when I was a college student and needed a job. I thought manning her desk as she did the work of racial justice with churches and universities was a dream come true. Turned out the real gift was my ongoing relationship with her. I wouldn't meet Gail for many years, but as with Brenda, I felt from her an instant connection and a protectiveness over me that I could not resist.

Often their care for me comes in the form of placing their hands on my face and asking if I'm *really* okay before I break down in their arms. Often their care for me is listening to me make big life decisions with all my fear and uncertainty and a quivering voice. Often their care for me looks like sermons and advice and stories from their personal lives. But today it looks like letting me play.

We are having lunch and wander onto the topic of makeup. They know me well and are familiar with how my "church girlness" never really made space for my curiosity about cosmetics. I confess that I hardly wore makeup for my wedding. I dabbed on a little foundation, put on some shiny eye shadow, and added some lip gloss before walking down the aisle. It wasn't that I was disinterested in makeup. I just wasn't clear how my training as a "good, modest girl" could make space for it. And there are so many rules for girls. You can wear some makeup, but only if it looks "natural." Put on too much and you're trying too hard. Put it on the wrong way, and you'll be talked about for not being on trend. Don't put any on and you might regret those photos. It was a lot to navigate, and I mostly opted out. By the time I broke free from those expectations, I felt so behind it was embarrassing.

Enter the bright idea. Brenda and Gail look at each other and chime, "We are going to Sephoras." (You know we put an *s* on the end of everything!) They pay for lunch and off we go.

I am a bundle of nerves. I get nervous walking into hair salons. Now I was going to walk up to a makeup artist and attempt to convey what I wanted? It felt a little impossible, but I really, really wanted to do it. I wanted to be made up. I decide not to deny myself this small pleasure—despite my nervousness. I grab hold of Brenda's and Gail's hands on the way in.

They take care of everything, these two women who are not shy. They announce that we need my makeup done and we want the works. They stay with me while I wiggle in the chair. They ooh and ahh when the woman comes back with a basket full of products to begin painting my face.

It feels so weird. The brushes keep tickling my cheeks. I can't stop flinching when she gets near my eyes. "You don't do this very often, do you?" she asks.

"No," I admit, "this is actually my first time getting my makeup done."

"Well, I'm honored," she responds kindly. "And don't worry about your body's natural reaction. The more you do this, the more your body will relax."

I smile without speaking as she draws my lips, hoping she can sense my gratitude for not making me feel like a complete weirdo. She takes the opportunity to explain what she's doing and why. She uses the concealer to cover my red spots. She makes my eyes appear wider by using a wing. She explains the technique she is using for my eyebrows. It's a crash course I am grateful for.

And then she is done. I look at Brenda and Gail for affirmation. Their eyes are wide. They blink at me, hands covering their mouths, for a moment without words. Then simultaneously, they let out high-pitched squeals and encourage me to turn to the mirror.

When I see my reflection, I am stunned. I am glowing, actually glowing. My eyes shine brighter and somehow appear darker. I am taking notice of their shape, the way they curve across my face. My lips, which I've been told are completely undefined and would make wearing lipstick difficult, are full and round. My cheekbones are high and my eyelashes long enough for me to see without the mirror. It's incredible.

Afterward Brenda and Gail split the makeup in half and pay for all of it. That stash became the foundation of my freedom to play. I started playing with my style—trying on clothes I thought I'd never like. I returned to my love for grommets and zippers, and this time I was completely confident in my choices. Turns out I actually like my bell-bottoms *bigger*. I started playing with jewelry, finding ways to wear it without breaking out. I started playing with my hair, wearing my curls more often instead of always tying them down into braids. I took off the heels I felt expected to wear onstage and put on tennis shoes. Before I knew it, the little girl who rocked black-and-white-striped bell-bottoms in elementary school started to reemerge. She started to glow again.

Being makeup-free was supposed to prove to myself and everyone that I was not self-important, self-focused, or self-absorbed. In truth, a whole piece of my self-exploration had been missing, because avoiding makeup wasn't my personal choice. It was someone else's. And when two women who I adore gave me permission to play, I both found new versions of myself and returned to old versions I will never hide again.

Therapy

FOR YEARS I repress the memory of shivering in the shower. I tell myself that I'm not a shower person, that I don't love showers as much as other people seem to, that I'm just a ten-minute-shower kind of girl. But during the pandemic, I have time to read a number of self-help books. One of them contains quizzes about my childhood. As I'm lying in bed answering the questions, I remember. I remember what happened to me in the shower. I remember that my avoidance of shower stalls is not about preference but about fear and anxiety. I remember but, at the same time, I lack the language for expressing what happened to me. And unlocking the memory doesn't stop the fear from rising the next time I step into the shower stall.

I need a therapist. And I find an incredible Black woman, UC, who gently walks with me to the other side of my trauma. UC helps me recognize that my body has deemed showers dangerous. Every time I take one, I am asking my body to risk going back to that danger zone. And present in that shower stall with me, present all the time, is not just the humiliating, nonconsensual critique I received in the shower stall—it's everything I learned about modesty, and sexuality, and sensuality, and control, and religion, and instructions on how not to be fast. It's all there. The conditioning. The pain. The church. The repression.

It takes several sessions just to help me put it all together. Eventually I invite my husband into the process, because it feels important for him to understand the journey I'm on. During our first combined session, Tommie confesses that he really wants to save me. He wants to save me from the pain. He wants to ride in on his horse and scoop me up and make sure I feel safe forever. It's so sweet.

My therapist leans forward and in a gentle but firm voice says, "Austin will save herself."

Her words settle into me, I feel them breaking me wide open. "I will save myself," I whisper. "I will save myself."

Over the next two months, as I make the turn from understanding to empowerment, my therapist helps me answer the question *What do I need to feel safe?*

I begin with the cosmetic, with making the bathroom feel like it's mine. I put up watercolor artwork—soft, ethereal, inviting. I add candles. Lots of candles. I pile them high on a cake stand, making them the focal point of the bathroom counter. I hang a shelf and fill it with items that are soft or smell good or are pretty. I put a small lamp on the other side of the counter to cast a yellow light across the room. I feel less exposed in the mild darkness.

Then she encourages me to think about everything that my body will touch. How do I create a tender experience for myself? For a little bit I buy only the expensive shower gel, the one with the scent that I absolutely love, the only one that feels like it might actually transport me somewhere else. I leave the loofahs behind, opting for thick washcloths that feel gentle on my skin. I order a small heater, specifically for use in a bathroom, and turn it on. My body has an easier time adjusting to getting in and out of the shower surrounded by warmth from that small heater. I don't shiver quite so much when I open the door to step out of the stall.

My therapist keeps encouraging me. What else would make you feel safe? What else would help you look forward to being in that space?

I ask my husband for help. "Babe, do you mind if I lock the door?" I need to know that no one is going to walk in on me. My husband and I walk in on each other all the time. It usually doesn't matter—except when I'm in the shower. And my little boy is still learning the word "privacy." He means no harm, but I don't want to scare him if I happen to get triggered when he opens the door and waltzes in. My husband agrees and keeps the baby occupied while I shower, so that there are no unexpected visitors.

My therapist invites me to reconsider every detail of how I shower. If I get anxious while washing, she suggests I try lightly running water over those areas. Treat them kindly. Aim for what makes me feel good about how I'm treating myself. She encourages me to explore water temperatures. Maybe I don't want the water to be hot; maybe I'll like it lukewarm or even cold. It's okay for it to be what I want it to be.

The first time I enjoy taking a shower, I am overcome by

emotion. I don't need the lock forever. My body learns to calm down.

All of these changes make it possible for me to confront my anxiety, to move through it. But I'm not done yet. I still have to work on the voice in my head. The one that critiques me. An anxiety specialist teaches me to kick the critic out of the bathroom. To take big breaths. To remind myself that no one is here to tell me what to do. It may sound sacrilegious, but I start repeating to myself, "This is my body. This is my body. This is my body." The words begin to heal me; they empower me to listen to my own voice.

My healing is still under way. But my therapist was right. Austin is saving herself.

Water

I ALWAYS THOUGHT skinny-dipping was a white people thing. I mean, who else could get away with going completely bare in places where that is not explicitly permissible? When white couples do it on TV shows and in movies, it's pretty clear they have no fear of getting caught, or offending someone, or the million and one scenarios I can think of for why this would be a bad idea for Black people. You really have to be in the moment, you know? But being in the moment for Black people is usually reserved for our homes—places we can control. For us, being in the moment is not for public spaces.

So, how did I end up defying my own expectations? Well, of course it started with some white people.

I should clarify, not only white people. Our little squad was "diverse." Age, race, Christian tradition, size, sexuality, where we lived, family structures—we were all over the place. Most of us were pastors or ministers, but this isn't your normal church group, okay? The only two things we all had in common were that we were owners of vaginas and all had one matching tattoo. There were ten or so of us, and twice a year we would get together for a weekend retreat.

The very first time we got together was in Denver, for a naked spa day. It was at turns both transcendent and grounding to be surrounded by naked women—young women, gray-haired women, big butt women, small breast women, unshaven women, tattooed women—all walking around freely, enjoying the spa services, smiling at one another and chatting as if being naked with strangers was perfectly normal. It was incredible.

After that, we decided (okay, maybe I decided) that every retreat would include "nekkid time" together.

So, there we were. Our white cargo van pulling up to a beach house right on the ocean in Florida. I heard someone shout from the back, "Skinny-dipping for naked time!" My mouth fell open. *Skinny-dipping?* Listen, I felt quite a wave of feminine freedom at the spas we had chosen before, but it was also safe and expected that we would all get naked there. There were no windows. Now, our foray into nude togetherness would be skinny-dipping on a public beach? *Oh nooo.*

For the next three days, this delightful group of women pastors, vocalists, writers, artists, and professors ministered to one another. We sang hymns while staring out at the sunset. We danced around the kitchen singing every word to Beyoncé's "Sorry." We practiced yoga together, cooked meals together, and cuddled together, whispering the secrets we could not publicly share—divorces and dating, children in crisis, new job interviews, plans for moving. Despite our titles, we were a collection of misfits for sure, and I loved every second of snuggling and sharing and praying and singing and eating and laughing . . . so much laughing with them.

And then we were down to our last day together. Some of our group had already taken a dive into the water in just their birthday suits. I wasn't one of them. But with the trip winding down, I reflected on the fact that every time I was with these women, I found myself doing something wild—something I never imagined. They were expanding me. They were giving me a gift that few Christians get to experience; instead of closing off the world to me, they opened it wide. There was never peer pressure, just a warm, joyful invitation to meet myself in a new way. I decided to take it.

"Okay! I'm in!" I shout at no one in particular. I shed my clothes in the living room in front of the wide sliding doors I need to walk through to get to the ocean. I can see four or five of my friends, naked bodies bobbing in the water. I look down at my own body.

It had changed so much over the years, but especially after giving birth to my beautiful son. He seemed to think it was appropriate that we both emerge from the experience with plenty of chubby. Until giving birth, I was totally unaware of how much my sense of self was rooted in being small. My mother used to call me the human clothes hanger because whenever we went shopping, everything always fit. Now, my body was different. There was no snapback for me. I was all stretch. Everything is wider—my hips, my thighs, my arms. And I had the sneaking suspicion that I was never going back to what was.

With all of my insecurities and fears and new rolls, I walk out onto the sand, the sunlight overhead providing just enough warmth for me to not hightail it back inside. I am aware of every sound outside, most notably the construction workers on top of the roof just a few houses down.

The sand stretches on entirely too long. How many more steps to the water? I am starting to regret this idea when another Black woman takes my hand. Also naked and brimming with confidence, she winks at me. Together we walk the rest of the way until we can finally put our toes in the surf.

"Ahhhhh!" we shout at the same time. Did I mention it's December?

The frigid water beckons us to come closer, even as it punishes us for doing so. We are up to our ankles, and then my body can't move. A receding wave takes the sand under my feet, burying them deeper where I stand. The rush of cold sends shivers up my body. It remembers shivering. I am cold and trembling and exposed. I cannot move. I'm frozen in place.

My friend waits. She holds my hand and she waits. I take a deep breath and ask myself, *Do you want this?* And the answer is yes. Yes, I want to experience all this moment could have for me. I want to experience it here, right now, with these women.

I take a step forward. And then another. And another. The water is back to our ankles,

then our knees,

then our thighs,

then . . . HOLY SHIT.

I'm a writer, and I still don't have enough words for the feeling that comes next. It is stunning and shocking. Talk about feeling a l i v e. My friend and I stop walking and at the same time, slowly turn toward each other. Both of our eyes are wide with the same question, *Do you feel that?*

Then laughter. Loud, unadulterated squeals of laughter and delight. Our hands, now free, form tight fists in an attempt to contain the surprise and the cold sensation slowly climbing up our bodies. More four-letter words follow as we reach for any verbal communication that can describe the water's impact. Every few steps all we can do is stand perfectly still until our brains tell our legs to keep walking.

We grab hands again and slowly submerge our bodies, letting go only when we have to balance ourselves. Eventually we make it all the way to our necks and stand alongside the group already playing among the ripples.

I close my eyes and turn my face toward the warmth of the sun, lifting my feet so that I'm floating in the water. I am listening to the voices of my girlfriends, the voice of the wind, the voice of the water, and the delight of my own body.

I am shivering again. But this time is different.

Remember this, I plead with my body. *Remember all of this.*

My body remembers trauma. It remembers tears and grief. It remembers rage and anger, danger and pain. But I believe it also remembers joy. I believe it also remembers healing. If my body is keeping the score, it is calculating not only what went wrong but what has been beautiful and inviting and thrilling and bursting with love. I am writing the story of myself, and I'll be damned if there won't be more romances and more adventures and more solidarity—and, yes, more justice work. But this time, it will be rooted in the life I want for myself. If I am to be undone by life, let it be a beautiful undoing.

Acknowledgments

THANK YOU TO THE CONVERGENT TEAM FOR BELIEVING in this book, especially Theresa Zoro, Gail Gonzales, and Tina Constable. To the marketing team, Jess Foggy and Rachel Tockstein, and Alisse Goldsmith-Wissman in publicity, thank you for your belief in this book and the passion you brought to this project. Thank you to Jessie Bright for bringing the title to life in this beautiful cover, Barbara Bachman for designing the pages, and to production editor Ada Yonenaka. And of course, thank you to my editor, Derek Reed, who had to put up with so much of my whining. Ashley C. Ford, what a blessing it is to know and love you, Sister. Thank you for your labor in writing this foreword. And to my literary agent, Margaret Riley King, you believed I could do this long before I was convinced. Thank you for always seeing me so clearly and believing in me so fiercely.

This is by far my most vulnerable piece of writing to date, and it simply would not have been possible for me to present these stories without the support and encouragement of so many people. Shout out to my therapists (yes, plural) without whom I would still be disconnected from myself. Thank you to the former board of Together Rising who had brilliant answers for me when I was struggling to define this project. To my unofficial editors Jeff Chu, Lisa Ann Cockrel, and Glennon Doyle, thank you for believing this could be something when it was still an absolute mess. Thank you to my beta readers who made me feel less crazy by shouting, "Me too!"

To my family, thank you for never getting tired of listening to me talk about this project. I imagine it's a little scary having a writer in the family, and it means the world that you trust me with our stories. To my girls Steph, Brooke, Jenny, and Amena, I would not have made it through these pages without being able to process with you. Thank you for the numerous ways you show up for me. And, of course, to my partner, Tommie, who had to listen to me unpack in vivid detail every story here along with the other fifty that didn't make it. The ways you care for my heart amazes me every day. Thank you for making it possible to write by being the best dad to our little boy and my biggest supporter in so many tangible ways.

I will never get over how many people it takes to create a book, distribute it, and get it into the hands of readers. All my life books have been my safe haven, and that's only possible because of the printers, the boxers, the truck drivers, the stock people, the bookstore owners, the librarians, and all of you whose fingerprints are on every single copy of every single book.

And finally, to every Black woman who has loved me well, I thank you with my whole heart.

AUSTIN CHANNING BROWN is an author and speaker providing inspired leadership on racial justice in America. She is the *New York Times* bestselling author of *I'm Still Here: Black Dignity in a World Made for Whiteness,* a Reese's Book Club pick. Her writing and work have been featured by outlets such as *On Being, Chicago Tribune, Shondaland,* and WNYC.